It's over for the United States economy we must change course and survive or go the way of the Great Auk. Now, only abolishing the minimum wage law can save the USA economy from total doom. It's too late for cutting spending to save this economy now only the abolishment of the minimum wage law can save the USA and world economy from total doom.

I0469935

The truth of the whole matter is government as a family provider on a mass scale has never been done in the history of mankind even during the days of slavery. Cutting spending would just mean a smaller welfare state and a smaller pie to share. And would just speed up the demise of this joke of an economy we have today. Its too late now, there is no turning back, we are pass the

point of no return, end of story, that is all she wrote, only abolishing the minimum wage law can free us now to save ourselves. We have already entered the early stages of total doom when we are printing tons and tons of

worthless currency in digital form.
Sure, they say we have been saved
from going over the so called physical
cliff.

It is very simple, to save the USA
economy now the free market place
must be set free, nothing else can do
it. Even when the free market place is
set free it will take an all out struggle
just to survive. That is because the
welfare state has already destroyed
practical everything that makes
civilization work.

No civilization or society has ever
survived very long without a strong
nuclear and extended family system, a
strong religious and moral code in
place, and emergency fallback
bartering capacity with plenty of small
farmers and home gardeners.

The main reason why the three said
survival tools is a must is the boom
and bust cycle is part of nature and
sooner or later the bust side of the
cycle must complete it rotation. And I
will guarantee anyone that there is no

way in hell the USA is going to survive unless we abolish the minimum wage law where the free market place can give us a fighting chance to survive this monster size bust cycle on the horizon.

With my God given super natural wisdom I'm telling you we must abolish the minimum wage law now before it is too late. Concerning the Minimum wage law almost everyone is focused on wages and salaries only, but that is obviously shallow thinking and the reason the welfare state is out of control.

The real not so obvious disguised poison fang the minimum wage law has is it gives the welfare state almost absolute power over the free market place. By being able to set and control the price of labor that also gives the welfare state control over private property too and what you can do with it. After the republicans caved on the over the cliff deal the Dems and liberals are licking their chop about this big harvest of new revenue to grow more government. However, I think they may be disappointed. I wouldn't be one bit surprised if the government ends up taking in less revenue than it is currently taking in.

Human being is not just cogs in some giant machine. Rich and successful people are not stupid, sooner or later they are going to get fed up with being used and abused and make a drastic change in behavior. Why should they continue to make great personal sacrifices to feed a thankless hostile welfare state to be spit upon and abused?

I'm telling you the rich and successful people are the life blood of this nation and are the one that make it work. Only ignorant people, freedom haters, and wanna be dictators puts down and tries to destroy the rich. No matter how hard the great depression was no one set out to scape-goat and destroys the rich.

No matter who does it, they don't love freedom or this nation if they try to

turn the masses against the very
people who make this nation work.
That is biting the hand that feeds you
and is un-American in my view.

There never has been and never will be
a rich and prosperous county without a
lot of rich people to make it happen.
Why you think almost the whole world
is poor and will always be poor, they
won't allow but a handful of people to
become rich. The USA is still the
economic engine of the world, if the
USA goes down the dragons and little
dragons would be in the poor house
within weeks.

The economic mess the USA is in there
is no managing your way out because
there are just too many variables. The
only way out is to simply abolish the
minimum wage law and just set back
and watch the free market work its
magic.

However, since the welfare state has
all but destroyed the nuclear and
extended family and everything else.
To protect the poor government must

establish govern run commissaries,
housing, and clinics and use tokens or
script for all who qualify.
SIRMANS LOG: 14 JANUARY 2013,
1957 HOURS

THIS ATTACK THE RICH LIBERAL
CLASS WARFARE BULL SSSS IS
DESTROYING THIS GREAT COUNTRY
AND IS UN-AMERICAN AND SICK IN
MY VIEW.

"GOOD GOVERNMENT IS A
PROTECTOR NOT A PROVIDER!"

*(HAPPY 70TH BIRTHDAY FREDDIE L.
SIRMANS, SR. BORN DECEMBER 22,
1942 IN STOCKTON, GEORGIA USA)*

EMERGENCY SURVIVAL PLAN FOR
AMERICA BEFORE TOTAL DOOM!
For a few years now I have kept up a
constant drum beat to get rid of
the minimum wage entirely, to rip it up
by the root and burn it to never return.
Well, almost no one understands that
and can't see the logic of my thinking
on this.

The thing about the minimum wage that makes it so destructive to a free market capitalism system is the fact that it is socialism to the core. The truth is it gives the government almost absolute power and control over private property and our free enterprise capitalist system of government.

In fact a free market place ceases to exist when any government sets wage control over private property owners. It doesn't matter if it is one penny or one hundred dollars you decide to pay as long as it is your private property, the government should butt out.

That is why practical all taxes should be on real property or something physical. Any time government controls production and distribution of what you can do with your own private property that is flat out socialism no matter how much they say it is free market capitalism.

In fact this whole matter of a minimum

wage to me is not so much about
wages but the power it gives
government to control private property
and what one can do with it. This
whole big government welfare state
spins off government's ability to
control private property through a
minimum wage.

The ability of government to set any
wage is the true reason the growth of
government is impossible to stop. I will
repeat, if this great nation is to survive
the minimum or any government wage
control must be eliminated, period.

It is very simple, I understand the
inner workings of an economy as well
or better than most people. No one no
matter how learned can truly
understand economic unless they
understand its basics which are trade
and bartering first.

Trade and bartering kept people alive
and has existed long before a currency
was invented. It is simple we don't
have enough people producing and
growing at least some of their own

food. Mass hunger and starving is going to be the end result of all this worthless money the government is printing up.

With this welfare state at this late stage and the course we are on it is ridiculous to even consider getting out of debt, just being able to survive as nation should be the first priority. With the course we are on we will continue to become worse off until a total collapse occur, it is simply inevitable.

My logic is with the course we are on it would be nice to plan on getting out of debt but that is a pipe dream. We must first change course and fight to survive at all cost. I guarantee you it is impossible to save this great nation as a welfare state, period. And I don't give a damn what the learned egg heads or anyone else tells you.

I know beyond a shadow of doubt that the welfare state cannot and will not survive, period. Now, it is down to the people having to save themselves and the nation, the government cannot and will not save this great nation.

More tax money and bigger
government will just speed up the day
of reckoning, which will be more and
more worthless money until the whole
thing collapse. That is why when I tell
you the minimum wage law must go I
know what I am talking about.

The elimination of the minimum wage
entirely is our only hope of surviving as
a free nation. Eliminating the minimum
will set the free market place free to
work its magic and save this great
nation.

Eliminating the minimum wage will
break the deadly choke hold big
government and the welfare state has
on free enterprise and the free market
place. Without the minimum wage, it
will allow the citizens the freedom to
barter and hire each other as maids,
handy man service, or whatever to eat
and survive.

As it is now with a minimum wage the
average citizen can't hire anyone

without wage control and mountains of red tape, why bother. The people must be set free of any kind of wage control for this great nation to survive and that is without a doubt, period.

Anyone with an ounce of economic sense knows that we can't survive much longer with the course we are on. Every day this nation is printing tons of worthless money and with that going on even an idiot should know that soon money won't be worth the paper it is printed on.

Still, this welfare state beast we have is doing it damnest to grow more government and create more dependents, that is insane, and don't belong in the real world of reality. These hoards of people will be left with no ability to survive on their own, and to me that is a crime against nature.

But, I have no power except my pen to try to bring some sanity to bear. Hopefully my advice will be taken and the minimum wage will be eliminated entirely. But, it doesn't end there the

poor and disadvantage has to be
protected.

They no longer have the nuclear and
extended family umbrella that always
stood guard until the welfare state
took away that survival need. When
this welfare state soon collapses they
must have a lifeline.

So, when the minimum wage is
completely gotten rid of the poor and
disadvantaged still must never be
completely abandoned. The first order
of business is the government must
establish government runs
commissaries, housing, and clinics and
use tokens or script for all who qualify.

This must be done to keep guaranteed
government handout money from
contaminating and destroying the free
market place as it is now. That is
another reason why I know this
welfare state economy can never be
saved.

What is happening with the economy
now is like feeding on you starting with

the big toe and continuing until there is no means to survive. We are eating our seed corn and drinking our priming water to wash it down; my God it is sheer insanity.

You just simply cannot have a lasting free market economy with government dumping tons of free unearned money into it. That is like the tax paying citizens paying to drive up the cost of living on themselves.

With the use of tokens, script, of whatever means government free unearned handout spending must be kept separated out of the free market place. That will stop the cost of living from inflating out of control like what is happening now.
SIRMANS LOG: 21 DECEMBER 2012, 1358 HOURS

THE SANDY HOOK ELEMENTARY SCHOOL CHILD KILLING
I try to stay away from making comments on matters like this because it is hard for me to pull punches. But, I

just had to say something and I will
make it very brief before getting into
too much trouble.

All focus is on the economy and
everyone seems to be ignoring the
inner fabric of this great nation, but,
I'm here to tell you that the liberal's
welfare state has almost completely
destroyed the nuclear family and eaten
away at the very fabric that holds
every society together.

Irresponsible parenting is at the head
of the list. Behavior is a result of what
one has been conditioned to be. You
can bend and shape a young sapling
but an older tree will break before it
will bend.

Every one is doting on the young like it
is just a love thing and it never
occurs to hardly anyone that a child is
suppose to be a responsible future
meal ticket and raised accordingly.
Almost every religion in the world
warns against worshiping self.

One must believe in someone or

something bigger than self to keep
from becoming a world into him. One
will never take his life or the life of
others if he has self-restraint for the
feelings of others. And that can be
taught, there is almost nothing innate
about a human being it is all a learned
experience.

I hear people complaining all the time
about not being able to enjoy a meal
at a restaurant or hear a good movie
because an unruly 5 or 6 year old is
out of control.

If a parent can't or won't control a 5 or
6 year old and repeat 50 times not to
do that, that parent in a reverse way is
actually teaching disrespect and
disobedience. Then at age 15 many of
these kids is lost forever, now whose
fault is that! How can you expect
someone to be responsible when they
have never been conditioned to be
responsible?

As far as to gun control, the shallow
minded liberals with their candy store
has all but destroyed this great nation

and knows an armed population is the only thing keeping them from making this a European style socialist state.

They want to get rid of all guns so bad they can taste it, and any excuse will do in their eyes. Thank God we have a second amendment standing guard over individual freedom in America.

Let me shut the hell up I have said too much already. PS: I think almost every social ill we have today can be traced to our liberal induced welfare state, period. I'm out of here.
SIRMANS LOG: 17 DECEMBER 2012, 2011 HOURS

A MINIMUM WAGE MUST BE COMPLETELY ELIMINATED, RIPPED UP BY THE ROOT TO NEVER RETURN.
I have tried to forget about my no "Minimum wage" crusade by thinking it will never happen. I have also thought about my continuing to write and why it seems like a waste of my time. But, it is like some invisible force that drives me to plod on, I'm not making

hardly any money at writing, yet, like a
zombie I keep marching on.

It has been said that many times when
destiny selects you for a mission it will
separate you from the crowd and make
you a loner. I have no monopoly on
one who has experienced a lot of pain
and suffering, but I believe I have had
more than my fair share.

So many things that the average
person takes for granted have been
mentally shut off to me, even if it's
just in my mind it is still just as real
to me. And almost as long as I can
remember it has been that way. I don't
think it is possible to become a saint
without experiencing great pain and
suffering. The movie "The Bells of
Saint Mary" showed that.

Like the old Negro spiritual says
(paraphrasing), nobody knows the
trouble I see, nobody knows my
sorrow. Many times pain and suffering
is an internal mental battle that can't
be seen by others but the destructive
damage is just as real.

However, the thing about pain,
hardship, struggle, and suffering is it
affects people in one or two ways. In
most cases it builds character and
turns one into a more caring human
being or maybe even a saint. But, with
a few it turns those into the most bitter
and evil human being one can imagine.

Enough on this I must get back to my
intended subject, in writing this article
I never intended to get side tracked off
into this entire Saint like stuff. It
seems as if my pen just took over as
character for a while and I had to
snatch it back.

Now, about me revisiting my "No
minimum wage" crusade. I truly
believe that the survival of the USA
and western civilization depends on
completely getting rid of a minimum
wage. If the minimum wage stays in
place I don't believe it is possible for
the USA or western civilization to
survive, period.

No matter what the egg heads in

Washington come up with it is impossible to save our welfare state. Their brains are scrambled, that is why they are called egg heads. Hell, anyone with a basic knowledge of economics should know that you can't get blood out of a turnip when none is there.

That same fact applies to food, money, or anything else, yet, these egg heads are making more and more people dependent on a well that is without a doubt about to dry up. It is sheer madness; even an idiot should understand that.

To continue doing something so shallow and stupid is a guarantee that there will be mass starving and social unrest that may take civilization all the way back to the stone age. Lord helps us.

The big enemy armored divisions of World War II ran on ball bearing and the strategy was to bomb the ball bearing factories out of existence. Well, the welfare state and big government power to control the free market place and private enterprise depends on having a minimum wage.

You can't have free enterprise or a free market place with government setting any labor price no matter how small or large. Sure, it was done in the name of helping the people like all social programs promised to do, but the Minimum wage gave a small baby welfare state a foot in the door and look at the beast we have today.

Any kind of government price or wage control over private production and distribution is a socialist or communist tactic and don't belong in our free enterprise capitalist system of government, period.

Of course, with no minimum wages people will earn less, but the things you buy would balance out and cost very little because business can never charge more than most people which are the poor can afford.

Getting rid of the minimum wage would stop all of this taxing everything

that one can imagine, and then taxing
would be limited to mostly real
property of some sort.

After completely getting rid of the
minimum wage, the next thing the
government must do is protect the
poor and disadvantage. And the only
way to do that without destroying the
free market place is for the
government to establish government
run commissaries, housing, and
clinics and use tokens or script for all
who qualify.

I promise you this USA and global
economy is about to blow and the only
way to bleed off the pressure is to
eliminate the minimum wage, period.
Otherwise, if they keep fiddling and
allow a total collapse no one knows
where it will end it may be all the way
back to the Stone Age.

If the USA keep fiddling and don't get
its duck all in a row this over the cliff
thing will be just the tip of the Ice berg
before total doom. I'm telling you not
to ignore my warnings because I can

dissect and understand an economy as well as anyone, just mark my words.

And another thing, these conservatives or anyone else out there that keep advocating big cuts in spending is out of their minds, it is too late for that.

They think they do but they don't truly understand economics. Sure, this economy is on the brink of a total collapse, but, with the mass amount of government dependents and debt load any drastic change in anything will instantly trigger the coming collapse right now, and no one wants that.

I, Freddie L. Sirmans, Sr. am suggesting the only course to save this great nation with freedom intact and prevent doomsday back to the Stone Age. The first thing that must be done is void and completely get rid of the minimum wage.

That will free up the people to save this great nation with freedom still intact, anything else is just buying a little more time. Getting rid of the minimum wage would allow the people themselves to save this great nation, which they can't do now because of the minimum wage and all kinds of government restrictions.

Big government and the welfare state can't save this great nation and have brought it to its knees and more taxes will just allow them to administer the coup de grace.

With no minimum wage to stop it the people can barter and hire each other as maid, handymen, or whatever to eat and survive, which they can't do now without wage and every other kind of government restriction. Soon millions will be starving sitting around waiting on government to save them.

Eliminating the minimum wage will allow the nuclear family to rebound and government can return to collecting taxes and protecting the country instead of snuffing out and lording it over the free market place.

Never forget the very poor and

disadvantage still need a life line, and to keep from contaminating the free market place the government must establish government run commissaries, housing, and clinics and use tokens or script for those who qualify.

Sure, a change like this would be traumatic, but, freedom and the nation would survive, whereas, anything else is still doomsday bound or just plain wishful thinking.

I hear all of these people out here running their mouths, but, in my view they are just repeating what someone else said or don't have a clue as how to dissect an economy like I can. SIRMANS LOG: 8 DECEMBER 2012, 2008 HOURS

FLIMFLAM GAME IS WHAT DEMS ARE TRYING TO PULL OFF CONCERNING THIS "OVER THE CLIFF" THING.
The weakness with the republicans is they are putting the country first and want to do the right thing. Whereas

that is the last thing on the minds of these dems and liberals, their first priority is to keep power by growing government and find a way to raise taxes and blame the resulting misery on the republicans.

I'm an independent, but that is why the republicans ought to tell them go fly a kite because we are never going to agree to raise taxes, period. But, doing that takes a lot of guts, and I for one am not sure the republicans have the guts to do that.

Besides, all of this "Lets make a deal" stuff is just a smoke screen by the Dems and liberals. Any one with an ounce of sense should know that the Dems and liberals are hard core tax and spenders, and never intend to cut spending or the growth of government under any condition no matter what they say.

There is no mystery about it growing government and doling out free goodies is what keeps them in power. Many times I have said that liberals were shallow and they are, but, I have never ever said that liberals were dumb.

Why do you think they have taken over and control almost every institution in this great free nation? Now, about this "Over the cliff" thing, the Dems and liberals have control of the reins, they really don't need the republicans for anything concerning this "Over the cliff" thing.

With one stroke of the pen the Dems and liberals leader can extend the Bush tax cuts at this very moment. But, there is a problem with doing that, doing that won't get them the tax increase and revenue they want to grow more government.

So, what they are really after is a way to kill two birds with one stone if they can make suckers out of the republicans. The way to do that is through negotiations, the two birds they are trying to kill is get their tax raise and blame it on the republicans at the same time.

They know the American public is dead set against a tax increase, except maybe on the falsely demonized rich. They also know that they can't successful blame the republicans unless the republicans themselves agree to some type of tax increase.

So, maybe if they can just keep pounding away on taxing the demonized rich hopefully the republicans will cave and agree to some kind of tax increase on the rich or something of the sort, and if they do. Bingo, they got their prey, it doesn't matter, and any agreed tax increase by the republicans should serve their purpose.

Then with their liberal cohorts in the news media everything will be distorted, twisted, and blown way out of proportion. Now, the Bush tax cuts will be allowed to expire and guess who agreed to a tax increase and in their eyes is a valid blame?

Sure, they were going to end up

blaming the republicans anyway but they see an agreed tax increase as the real thing. Now all you will hear is them mean old republicans who don't care about the poor or anyone, and is the reason for this big tax increase on the working people of America and on and on. It is the same old bait and switch liberal blame game strategy. SIRMANS LOG: 02 DECEMBER 2012, 1538 HOURS

WHERE IN THE "SAM HILL" IS THIS COTTON PICKING USA GOVERNMENT HEADED? CAPITALISM: Is where private property ownership and individual freedom thrives. Almost all production and distribution is privately owned and operated for a profit.

It is a system where profit rules the day and just about everything else, no profit means nothing for the government to tax and survive on. Profit can only be generated with some type of business transaction. All salaries and everything else the government taxes can be traced back

to the profit from some type of
business transaction.

When you attack the rich and
businesses you are attacking the very
source that generates the profit that
supplies the government with
revenue (money).

Right now the American businesses
can only generate 60 percent of the
profit needed for our government to
survive on, which means the
government is borrowing the other 40
percent.

Yet, these insane Dems and liberals
are hell bent on growing government
even bigger with more debt, my God!
This is sheer madness and twilight
zone stuff that fails every sanity test.
Maybe, it is
true that the Lord looks out for fools
and crazy people, we as a nation
are certainly going to need it.

As it stands most American businesses
are barely surviving, some has a
profit margin as small as 3 percent,

and with a margin that low a few employees stealing a few items will put them out of business.

Yet, these shallow minded Dems and liberals are hell bent on putting several more layers of taxes on these hard working job providers, Lord, what a crying shame. For every business that the government tax forces out of business that means more unemployment and less tax money to the government.

I'm telling you these shallow minded Dems and liberals are stacking on layer by layer of even more taxes thereby breaking the backs of businesses. And, in effect destroying this last great land of individual freedom. We may end up back in the Stone age and that is no joke.

Plus, what is even worse 95 percent of the American population is too economically ignorant to even have a clue as to what is going on right before their eyes. That is especially true with the learned shallow

surface dwelling predominate liberal
news media.

SOCIALISM: Is where private
ownership of property still exists but
the government controls the
production and distribution and what
you can
do with your private property.

COMMUNISM: Is where there is no
private property ownership and all
production, distribution, and ownership
is controlled by the government. And
in my view it leads to everyone being
equally poor except a privilege few,
unless there is vast natural resources
to sell on the open market.

If the Bush tax cuts are allowed to
expire I believe it will drive so many
businesses out of existance that the
USA government will end up taking
in far less tax revenue than it is taking
in right now.

IN CLOSING: The only way to save the
USA with our individual freedom
still intact can be found throughout the

writing of Freddie L. Sirmans, Sr.
SIRMANS LOG: 30 NOVEMBER 2012,
1541 HOURS

DOOMS DAY MAY BE NEARER THAN
WE THINK?
Here is my quick injection concerning
this so-called physical over the
cliff thing: This is sad for me to say,
but, I don't think the Dems and
liberals give a damn what financial
disaster awaits the USA as long as
they can stay in power and find a way
to blame it on the republicans.

When have a liberal ever accepted
blame and took responsibility for
anything unpleasant. Right now the
liberals holds the reins for the
safeguard and the direction this
country will take into the future, but to
listen to the bias liberal news media
you would think the republicans is
holding reins.

Here is what I think, I think the USA
house leaders ought to tell the
Dems, there won't be a tax increase on

the American people on our part
and then get the hell out of Dodge
(meaning any negotiations). The fact
is it is totally up to the Dems leader to
let the Bush tax cuts expire or
not.

So, go ahead, have your day, because
no matter what happens the
liberal media is going to blame the
republicans for everything that turns
out bad and nothing that turns out
good anyway.

We had better thank God there is some
resistance to these Tax and spend
liberals, just look at Detroit and most
of the northeast cities and the state of
California to see what happens when
liberals has no resistance and totally
have their way. Sure, on this over the
cliff thing the republicans are probably
going to as usually cave big time.

Which, will just add one more layer of
taxes on this nation and drive the
dagger in a little deeper toward the
heart and soul of this great nation?
Like a broken record I will repeat, our

welfare state cannot and will not
survival, and I don't care what any
learned anybody tells you, I'm
telling you it is impossible for it to
survive.

We will let history be the judge and I
believe the wait is on horizon
now. Mother Nature herself is not just
free wheeling it, Mother Nature
operates on set laws and the "Boom
and bust" cycle is a law of nature.

The USA and world economy is long
over due for a complete rebirth or
renewal bust cycle by Mother Nature.
There is no way man is going to
stop it, the rotation is life itself, there
is no life or existence for anything
without a cycle.

The wisest thing man can do is prepare
and get ready to try to survive
and live past it, the bust cycle is on the
horizon and the rotation must
be completed for new growth and life
to sprout anew. You will find the
right answers and correct course to
take throughout my writing, may

the Gods be with you, Gods speed.
SIRMANS LOG: 28 NOVEMBER 2012,
2104 HOURS

ANOTHER WORD OF WISDOM FROM
THE GREAT THINKER (ME), FREDDIE L.
SIRMANS, SR.
Most people are aware of the balance
factor concerning government
dependents on the dole becoming the
majority voting population. Well,
there is another balance factor that
even the learned economist may not
be keeping in mind.

This balance factor has to do with
paying taxes. It stands to reason that
no one is going to work if they are
taxed at 100 percent. So, that means
the government can tax up to a point
with very little behavior change in
the tax paying public.

But, once over a certain balance line
there is going to be a drastic
behavior change in the tax paying
public. I'll bet anyone a dollar to a
donut that we are on that line or even

a little over it.

That means if the Dems succeed in getting a huge tax raise or allow the Bush tax cuts to expire this USA government will end up taking in far less revenue than it is taking in now. Humans are complex beings that are motivated by a response to reward or punishment, which means no reward no motivation.

The liberals are too shallow to recognize the human factor; they see all
people as just cogs in some giant machine. Our rich and well to do job providers are fed up. They are not stupid, why should they keep making great sacrifices to just be beaten down, spit upon, and robbed of their hard earned money by a spendthrift government.

They know a fair amount of taxes must be paid but their money was earned and belonged to them, whereas the liberal media and big government believes all earnings belong to the

government and government is being
generous to give you a little back.

You mark my word from here on out
the more government taxes the
less revenue it is going to take in. Now
chew on that. In the authoritarian
countries they stress the punishment
side instead of the reward side to get
people to produce and use fear with
the promise if you don't work you don't
eat.

But, in free countries like the USA and
western Europe there is no longer
hardly any fear factor left, many
people get on the dole and will never
do hard labor, especially hot farm
labor.

So, I think in the coming months our
dole and food stamp population is
going to grow like a wild fire and drive
the final nail in the coffin of this
welfare state, or, at the very least
cause a lot of pain and suffering.
SIRMANS LOG: 18 NOVEMBER 2012,
1946 HOURS

THIS IS WHAT MUST BE DONE TO
SAVE THIS GREAT NATION. ALSO,
THIS IS THE RERUNNING OF THIS
ARTICLE.
The reason why I don't think the polls
will move very much in Mitt's
favor is because we live in a welfare
state which means we have masses
upon masses of government's
dependents that believe in big
government mind, body and soul.

And their one and only focus and
interest is "What has government
done for me lately." These dependents
are bonded to the Democratic
Party like a child is bonded to its
mother.

That means these dependents will
never be swayed with reason and
logic, some where along the line an
indelible stamp was put on their
brain that the republicans is the
enemy. And the only thing that can
remove that stamp is to become an
independent thinker.

However, no dependent thinker volunteers to become an independent thinker they must be forced to fend for themselves to become an independent thinker. All of that means these big government dependents are going to emotional support and vote democratic no matter how their candidate performs.

That is why I think it is short sighted to chase after people who will never vote republican under no condition, instead I think they should be pounding and pounding to no end lower taxes across the board, more jobs, and strong national defense with no regret, anything else only creates class envy.

It is very simple, if the republicans can't win with lower taxes "The inmates has already taken over the asylum" anyway. So, in the grand scheme of things, my final analysis is what do it really matter who win the election both candidates is determine to try to save save the welfare state.

In my view the welfare state is over done for and need to be buried, I think it is impossible for the USA and western civilization to survive unless the welfare state is abandon, period. Also, I think anyone that thinks the welfare state can be saved can't possible understand the free market or economics, period.

I may be wrong about a lot of things but without a doubt in my mind I know the welfare state can't possible be saved. With the damaged it has done to western civilization we will be lucky if we survive at all without going back to the Stone Age even if we abandon it today.

Otherwise Mother Nature is on the brink of stepping in herself, and I will tell you now if we don't act now a totally economic collapse is going to happy any day now. Unless my super natural wisdom advice is heeded western civilization is doomed in my view.

Yes, little old me has the answer.

Again here is my survival solution, first get rid of the minimum wage entirely, rip it out by the root. Next, establish government run commissaries, housing, and clinics and use tokens or script for the poor, disadvantage, elderly, or whoever qualifies for aid.

Third void all taxes accept enough property tax for national defense, interior, and the operation of government, because it is going to come to that anyway when this economy soon totally collapse.

Forth, Government get the hell out of the free market, stay with collecting the taxes due, protecting and defending the country, and then the American people will save themselves and the government, too. But, to continue with this nanny state we have no chance of continuing to survive, period.

Hell, I know I'm not going to be taken serious, but, I'm a writer and I writer what I think, I can't make anyone believe or act upon anything I

write, but, believe it or not at least it is
food for though. And while I'm
at it, another thing, everyone thinks
the boom and bust cycle is a bad
thing, wrong.

The boom and bust cycle is a law of
nature, and at some point the cycle
must be completed. I believe time has
finally ran out and the bust cycle
is answering the call of nature and no
matter what man does the bust
cycle is going to complete its rotation.

I think nothing man does is going to
stop it; I think all we can do Is
prepare to survive it. There are certain
things throughout history that only
Mother Nature's purges solved. Just
look around at the USA, the
anti-survival negative forces has just
grown too powerful and only
Mother Nature can bring them back
under control.

Just look at the moral decay, the lack
of family values, the murdering of the
innocent unborn in the womb and on
and on. When all of these negative

anti-survival forces like men marring men and women marring women and all the rest becomes the norm a country is ripe to be taken over, there is no way in hell it can survive long term.

So, if man can't or won't deal with the situation, nature's purges are sure to reset the clock. It has been proven in over 6,000 years of written history that the only way man can survive these purges of nature is with a strong nuclear and extended family system, a strong religious and moral code, and adequate emergency bartering capacity
with many small farmers and home gardeners.

Without these survival systems in place no civilization has ever been known to survive. Because of the "New deal" which birthed the welfare state, we have almost none of these survival systems left to survive nature's bust purge which is now coming upon us.

Our only hope is to act now before it

fully hit, then it may be too late for
the world. Lord, have mercy on the
USA.
SIRMANS LOG: 4 OCTOBER 2012,
1327 HOURS

IT IS INSANE TO GIVE A SPENDTHRIFT
MORE REVENUE (MONEY) EXPECTING
SOMETHING GOOD TO COME OF IT.
Giving a spendthrift more revenue
(money) expecting a cure to the
nation's financial problems is beyond
dumb and stupid it is sheer
madness.

The USA undoubtedly is living in
fantasy land because in reality when
you are 16 trillion in debt and still
growing government you must be
suicidal or have some kind of psychotic
death wish. These liberals has
gone stone mad.

I know as rule liberals are shallow with
weak survival instincts, but, the
American voters just recently gave
them the reins and there is no way
to snatch the reins from them. So, off

the nations goes in full gallop into
financial wonderland and shaking them
won't work because this is not a
dream.

I want to laugh but I can't because this
is not a laughing matter we are
all in this wagon as it heads toward the
cliff. I'm trying to snatch the reins in
my writing but who the hell ever heard
of Freddie L. Sirmans, Sr. and even if
they did, my type of cure would be
bitter medicine and this nation is not
about taking any of it without going
through a lot of hardship and suffering
first.

When you see businesses and
individuals making extreme profit and
huge salaries that is because of big
government and the welfare state.
That is mainly due to lack of
competition. You see, no matter what
the shallow minded liberals may tell
you, only local, state, and the federal
government has the power to keep out
the competition.

This is done with all kind of codes,

licenses, fees, permits, regulations, etc. Sure, standards and qualification is needed but it don't end there the overkill is to keep out competition and the small guy.

Big government and big business scratches each others back, big business use government to price out competition and big government uses big business to push its social engineering agenda. However, big business can't force anybody to do anything whereas the government can.

Sure, big business has financial power and the money to pay huge teams of Philadelphia lawyers for awesome civil power, but that is about all.

My overall view is unless this government goes back to being a last resort for the poor and disadvantage where the nuclear family can rebound this great land of individual freedom will not survive as a free people, period.

As to the "Physical over the cliff" thing,
my gut feeling is the republican house
will end up caving, my God what a
shame, but it is what it is. I could go
on and on but I think you get my drift
as to the state of the nation in my
view.
SIRMANS LOG: 17 NOVEMBER 2012,
1420 HOURS

ANALYSIS OF THE 2012 PRESIDENTIAL
ELECTION
First, here is a word of wisdom from
the great thinker, you see, the
general public as a whole has a herd
mentality and really don't know
what the hell they truly want.

The founding fathers were aware of
this fact and that is the main
reason we have a republic form of
government. A republic is designed
to select people that will lead not fall in
line to follow an uninformed
economic illiterate mob like herd with
the use of insane polling.

There is no wonder why this nation

may go over the cliff. Failing to realize this fact is the main reason the GOP keep loosing and unless things change we are going to lose this great free nation, too.

I, Freddie L. Sirmans, Sr. the great thinker and self-made writer have decided to give my opinion on the 2012 USA presidential election.

I see all of the pundits and so-called political experts on TV trying to get the tag number of that truck that just ran over them. Dick, Carl, and a few others still haven't figured out what hit them. Well, I for one would have been surprised if Mitt had won. But, I admit that I too had been swayed with this "The polls are wrong" nonsense.

Now, let's get down to the brass tacks of the matter; I think Romney ran an insane blank slate campaign. And anyone who reads my website knows I said that long before the election. Ronald Reagan would never have run a blank slate type of campaign like that.

Romney's main focus was to just attack the other guy which was a waste of time and money. These government dependents don't give a damn what their candidate has done or what he looks like as long as he is the candy-man and will keep the handouts and goodies coming.

Plus, everyone already knows who the Dems are; the Dems are the candy man, Santa Claus, and uncle shugga. And that means that is around 47 percent of the voters who is going to vote democrat no matter what come hell or high waters.

To these voters color of race has nothing to do with it they are bonded to the Dems like mother and child; they believe the republicans are going to kick their crutch from under them. And believe it or not I agree with them, I think it is cruel to kick a crutch from under anyone before first giving them some kind of emergency support system.

So, the republican candidate started off with 47 percent already in the Dems column. But, he still has 53 percent to win with. So, my advice to the GOP is to focus mainly on the 53 percent of voters you have the best chance to get.

The voters the GOP has the best chance of getting are small business owners, home owners, and anyone who believes in lower taxes. But, on that I'm probably spiting into the wind, because in my view one of the dumbest and stupidest things Romney and the GOP did was to all but abandon lower taxes.

They flat out let the Dems and liberals lay a guilt trip on them by making them feel guilty and ashamed to believe in and fight for lower taxes for all. Not me, I believe taxes are already too high for everyone in this country and taxes should be lowered across the board.

I'm not hearing this class warfare bull

S**t, it is destroying this great country, and to me it is un-American and sick. If the Dems and liberals can't deal with it, tough titty, and to hell with them if they can't take a joke. Now, I have vented and cooled down.

All Romney had to do was pound and pound to no end lower taxes across the board, more jobs, and strong national defense. But, instead all he did was attack, attack, and head off in every direction and wallow in every controversial issue so no one really knew where he stood, and the votes he did get was "Anybody but Obama" in my view.

Believe me, I am not against Romney, what I'm writing may help someone else in the future. Romney now joins Dole and McCain as GOP presidential losers I believe because he too tried to out liberal a liberal for voters that will never vote republican under any circumstance.

There is no guarantee that what I

advocate will produce a winner, but, at lease the people will know what the candidate fought for. No one knows what Dole, McCain, or Romney fought for except to be president. So, to all of these people on TV wondering about the GOP's future, just keep the faith.

The Dems are going to self-destruct, give them enough rope and they will. Just look at California and all of the big cities in the northeast, all are almost in ruins. Whoa, I almost forgot, in my view the GOP has a macho element to contend with, I think this element put a lot of pressure on Romney to go for blood and attack , attack even just for the sake of attacking.

The downside to that strategy in my view is it is a loser strategy, because you can't get your own message out and define who you are then even your own base can trust you. Well folks, I condensed it greatly but that concludes my analysis of the 2012 USA presidential election. SIRMANS LOG: 11 NOVEMBER 2012, 1939 HOURS

REPUBLICANS MAY GET A SUPER MAJORITY IN BOTH HOUSES IN 2014! Here is something the liberals and Dems need to be aware of because of the so called looming physical economic over the cliff matter. This is something that can't be ignored and will determine if this great nation survives, period.

I think everyone knows that it is the Dems that is holding the reins. So, if the Dems botch this enough and cause enough pain and suffering all hell could break lose. After all the American voting public is a very fickle bunch and right or wrong has a herd instinct.

This physical cliff thing is no piece of cake and there is no easy way out left, the Dems are going to have to make some hard choices or face disaster.

A big enough screw up on this by the Dems could make the voters mad

enough to award the GOP super
majorities in both houses of congress
in
2014. And that would make the
president mostly a figure head after
that. So, my answer to all of this is:
Just the facts maam, just the facts.

I'm just saying, this is something the
Dems should just be aware of. Hell, I
know the Dems are experts at blame
shifting but in this case I doubt that
blame shifting will be enough to
placate the amount of pain
and suffering going on.

Seeing the writing on the wall and not
wanting to be entirely alone I look for
this administration to bring on board a
few Rockefeller type republicans.

I think they will look for big names like
Colin Power, Richard Luger, etc.
to put in high profile positions. That
way at the very least the republican
brand won't be entirely out of the
picture.
SIRMANS LOG: 8 NOVEMBER 2012,
1309 HOURS

THE DAY AFTER OBAMA'S WIN FOR
FOUR MORE YEARS ANALYSIS
I, Freddie L. Sirmans, Sr. great self-
made original thinking creative writer
maybe should keep my views on this
matter to my self, but, you know I'm
going to vent anyway.

I totally disagree with this
administration on almost everything. I
believe the president believes totally
the bigger the government the
better, and the government is the
answer to almost everything. I
believe he thinks government should
make sure everyone have an equal
chance for a job and every benefit this
country has to offer.

Now, on the surface all of the above
sound fair and reasonable, but that
is in theory. However, when actually
put into practice there is a fatal flaw it
that type of thinking, it doesn't work.
It has never worked and never will for
a simple reason, humans are not cogs
in a machine.

Humans are complex emotional beings
that are motivated by a response
to reward or punishment, period. So,
that being the case it means all of
the president's policies now and in the
future will never work in practice and
are guaranteed to fail. But, never lose
faith; there is a much bigger picture
and message hidden here.

In my view the president is no ordinary
man; I believe he is a man of destiny.
I believe he truly wants to do what he
feels is fair and best for all Americans
all though I totally disagree with his
method.

So, no Democrat would have dared
open the door to China, but,
republican Richard Milhouse Nixon did
it. So, no republican will dare break the
back of our welfare state, but,
democrat Obama is going to do it if
that is what it takes to save this great
nation. "The Lord works in mysterious
ways."

Disagree or dislike Obama if you must

but this is a man who knows what it feels like to be different, looked down upon, or maybe even ridiculed. He has said many times "If one is willing to work hard everyone should have the opportunity to succeed in America. Remember the words, "Work hard."

So, I'm warning all of you government dependents out there falling over yourselves with Obama mania, you had better wake up; Obama can be the real Obama now. I'm sure Obama believes in socialism
totally, but, I also believe this is a man that is not going to tolerate dead beat dads and people not working hard and pulling their share.

I believe the 'Lord works in mysterious ways." And this is a man guided by destiny and is here to break the back of the welfare state to save our nation whether he realizes it or not.

I, the great Destiny writer see a total economic collapse looming on the horizon. And for the sake of world balance, I don't believe Mother

Nature will let this great land of individual freedom perish from the face of the earth forever.

Agree with me or not, that is my analysis of what is playing our on the world stage starring the USA as protagonist.
SIRMANS LOG: 07 NOVEMBER 2012, 1401 HOURS

OBAMA WINS FOUR MORE YEARS! THERE IS AN OLD SAYING, BE CAREFUL FOR WHAT YOU PRAY AND WISH FOR BECAUSE YOU JUST MIGHT GET IT. THAT SAID, THE AMERICAN PEOPLE HAS SPOKEN AND CHOSEN WHO WILL LEAD US FOR FOUR MORE YEARS.

THE LORD WORKS IN MYSTERIOUS WAYS. HOWEVER, I AM FOR INDIVIDUAL FREEDOM AND RESPONSIBILITY AND NOW BELIEVE THE WELFARE STATE INMATES HAS FINALLY TAKEN OVER.

WE AS A NATION ARE 16 TRILLION IN

DEBT, WHAT'S UP WITH THAT.
HOW MUCH OF OUR FREEDOM AND
SOVEREIGNTY WILL BE SOLD OFF
JUST TO TRY TO SAVE OUR
UNSAVABLE WELFARE STATE?
SIRMANS LOG: 6 NOVEMBER 2012,
2341 HOURS

LURKING ON THE HORIZON IS A
TOTAL WORLDWIDE ECONOMIC
COLLAPSE!
As I, Freddie L. Sirmans, Sr. self-made
great writer put pen to paper
here on the eve of the big dance,
meaning the 2012 USA presidential
election. I'm just going to repeat what
I have said before.

In the grand scheme of things it really
doesn't matter a hill of beans who win
this beauty contest. The reason why I
believe this is because both candidates
are hell bent on trying to save our
welfare state, which I know is
impossible. I don't care what the hell
the learned economist or anyone else
tells you, I'm telling you now it can't
be done it is impossible, just keep

living and you will see for yourself.

Now, here is the way it's going down, if
the Dems win we can kiss
individual freedom in the USA good by.
And brace for the selling off of
what's left of USA sovereignty. Also,
I'm sure the Dems are going go all
out for a complete power grab to gain
absolute power for the welfare
state.

As to the economy, the Dems will do
nothing to prevent or prepare for
the coming total world wide economic
collapse, simply, because they
are too shallow to even think
something like that could possible
happen until it is too late. Now, on the
other hand if the GOP wins they will
head off in another direction but still to
no avail because the welfare state
can't be saved.

The GOP thinks they can put this
welfare state beast on a diet to keep it
from eating all of us alive, wrong. This
welfare state beast has grown to
strong and powerful for that and will

end up making the GOP look like
fools. In my view this beast is bloated
with years of rot, moral decay,
corruption, and inefficiency to the point
that it will never allow any real
rebirth and growth to save the USA.

This beast next step is going to be to
bite off the hand that feed it. We
all know that government survives on
the taxes it collects. But, what
few know and understand is that all
tax money comes from private
businesses and that is mostly small
businesses. Even home owners and
everyone else gets their income from a
private business sources profit.

It is simple; survival of government
depends on private profit, profit,
and more profit, with one exception
slavery or something like slavery.
Nothing the government does produce
a profit, only a private business
transaction can generate a profit.
Government can simply kill all
businesses just by taking to much of
their profit where they won't be
able to restock and pay others

expenses.

Being rich is an attitude and around
ninety percent of the people don't
have that attitude. Rich people are not
the same as poor people with
money, they have a whole different
mindset. There never has and never
will be a wealthy nation without a lot of
rich people to make it happen. Rich
people are the life blood of every free
nation that is why a dictator or anyone
against individual freedom will go after
and try to destroy the rich.

There is a reason why almost all of the
world is poor and will always be poor;
it is the crab syndrome, because those
in power will not allow a true free
market place. A government that
allows a free market place with free
competition and doesn't siphon off all
of the profit will never remain poor,
but, those in power almost never allow
that.

People are not stupid, no one is going
to work hard and produce a lot of
profit if government is just going to

take almost all of it away. That is
why socialism and communism always
make everyone equally poor
except a privilege few.

I can dissect an economy as well as
anyone, now, you are going to tell
me I don't know what the hell I am
talking about when I say the
welfare can't be saved, what a joke,
get real.
SIRMANS LOG: 06 NOVEMBER 2012,
0051 HOURS

ROUND #3 AND THE FINAL 2012
PRESIDENTIAL ELECTION DEBATE, A
QUICK BRIEF ANALYSIS BY ME,
FREDDIE L. SIRMANS, SR.
What the hell does it really matter, it is
all scripted anyway. Nothing is real
anymore as to what the candidate
really stands for, it is all fake and
window dressing driven by what
showed up on a poll, its fiction
and rehearsed, and whoever is the
most flamboyant with the best gift
of gab usually wins.

That is why the sages of old and the founding fathers almost to a man never trusted a democracy and is the reason we actually have a republic.

So, like I have said many times before, in the grand theme of things the welfare state can't be saved and both candidates is hell bent on trying to do just that, it is insane, trying to save the un-savable, what a joke, and sad situation in my view.

But, who cares what the hell I think! I'm seen as a nut case out here whistling Dixie, next patient please. SIRMANS LOG: 23 OCTOBER 2012, 0412 HOURS

UNDERSTANDING NATURE'S BOOM AND BUST CYCLES!
The boom and bust economic cycles in life is just like the life and death cycles, it is a necessity for long term survival. There is no escape from them because they are part of natures design.

Everyone seems to think that an
economy only involves money, wrong,
trade and bartering is the foundation of
every economy and has existed
long before a currency was invented.

Sure, a currency is an evolutionary
advancement in trade and bartering,
but, never forgets, you can't eat
material possessions, and it may come
a time when a garden and a shotgun is
worth more than two or three
million dollars.

Man can stave off the bust cycle, but
only so long and at a price, and
that price is the longer the delay the
greater the destruction when the
bust cycle rotation finally purges the
old to allow a new sprout to begin.

And in our case it may take civilization
all the way back to the stone age, but,
none of that has to happen if the USA
first get rid of the minimum wage
completely and follow other steps laid
out in my writing.

Right now we have almost no
emergency survival backup tools left in
terms of raw bare boned survival. All
throughout history a strong nuclear
and extended family system, a strong
religious and moral code, and
adequate emergency backup bartering
capacity with many small farmers and
home gardeners would keep us fed
through any bust cycle, like the great
depression. But, now almost all of
those tools has been destroyed by the
welfare state.

In terms of sheer survival we as a
nation have almost no chance of
surviving a total economic collapse, we
the USA and the civilize world may
very well go back to the stone age,
that is why I cry and preach so hard of
the wisdom of ripping out this
minimum wage demon to save our
nation.

The ripping out and complete
elimination of the minimum wage is a
start back to basics and the only thing
that is going to give this nation a
fighting chance and even that may be

too late. I can't stress the wisdom of
eliminating the minimum wage enough
no matter how sick and tired people
get of hearing it.

Just like death is not the end all, but
only one half of nature's life and
death cycle the same applies to
natures economic bust cycle. The
economic bust cycle looms on the
horizon, what are we the great USA
going to do to survive it.

For over 6000 years man has had the
same above said tools in place to
survive any economic bust cycle. But,
now starting with the "New deal"
that created our welfare state beast
those tools are very weak to
nonexistence. Time a wasting, what
are we the USA going to do, get rid
of the minimum wage or not, we must
prepare to stand alone if we must
because it's going to be every nation
for itself soon.

Maybe, we are going to just keep
fiddling and graciously accept going
back to the Stone Age. I pray we will

not, but I have no power except
my pen, and no one has to believe a
word I say, let along act on
anything I say.
SIRMANS LOG: 16 OCTOBER 2012,
1407 HOURS

FREDDIE L. SIRMANS, SR. OPENS UP
HIS SOUL TO HIS READERS FOR ALL
TO SEE WHAT MAKES HIM TICK
Folks I don't do this often and this is
the first time I have shared this
much of my inner self. In this brief
article I am going to talk only about
me. Sometimes I wonder what the hell
happened to me; I never set out
to be in any kind of political arena.

Why, why oh Lord, this is the last thing
that I ever wanted is to be in any kind
of public limelight. But, here I am as a
great raw crude self-made creative
writer commenting on the political
stage and being driven by some
unknown force to make my economic
and political views
known.

You see, all throughout my childhood I
suffered an inferior complex, but
some where deep down in my soul
there was a fighting instinct to
survive at all cost. No matter how
many times I was told that I would
never amount to anything I knew
different.

I never have and never will feel
completely comfortable and normal in
a
public setting. But, I'm still human and
cry, bleed, and feel pain the same as
other human beings. Also, I believe
that I have been blessed with
exceptional wisdom, talent, and ability
that very few appreciate or
understand.

I have no monopoly on past hardship
or suffering but I think I have
certainly had my share. No one can
acquire the deep wisdom that I
have without enduring a lot of struggle
in life. I don't attend church as
much as I should but I am spiritual to
the core.

I learned very young that those that can genuine love and forgive can never be mentally defeated. I believe genuine talent and ability is like a liquid in that it will always eventually seek it own level if one stay the course and never quit. I know the average reader will never understand my writing and most can't take it after a few paragraphs.

There is no reason for me to fret because if my ability and talent have what it take all of the kings horses and all the kings' men can't stop it from seeking its own proper level, and I will get my due. There, I have opened up my soul so my readers can judge the human side of me.

Sorry, if some see this as just plain self serving, but sometimes it is OK as far as I'm concern to just bare ones soul. This is insight into who I am and what I think.
SIRMANS LOG: 12 OCTOBER 2012, 1709 HOURS

I SEE A TOTAL ECONOMIC COLLAPSE ON THE HORIZON! A TOTAL ECONOMIC COLLAPSE LOOMS ON THE HORIZON, AND WHAT DO THE USA DO, FIDDLE WHILE ROME BURNS. When they win I'm sure the GOP plan on doing the normal good intention thing by balancing the budget, but, that can't be done in an out of control welfare state without growing the dole roll. Saving the welfare state is an impossible task.

Sure, your intentions are good, but, remember, "The road to hell is paved with good intentions." Doing the most sensible thing is what really counts, and it sure ain't trying to save an unsolvable burned out system.

I believe a total economic collapse is inevitable and is going to happen soon, no one knows when, hell, I have been pounding this same warning now for nearly twenty years. Still, no one listens or take my wisdom and warnings seriously.

Since we all know it is going to happen

and man can't stop it, I think the
wisest course is to prepare to
withstand and survive an all out total
economic collapse. Now, concerning
the upcoming presidential election,
I believe the GOP would preserve our
freedom and buy more time for a
miracle to come along and save us
from a total economic collapse.

But, now I'm not so sure anymore.
Under normal circumstance the GOP
would definitely buy us more time, but
the problem is we have a hungry
welfare state beast on our hands and
there is not enough money in the
entire world to keep it fed.

Both presidential candidates are hell
bent on saving the welfare state at
all cost and there lies the problem in
my view. I think trying to save the
welfare state is an impossible task and
economic suicide. We all know
with the Dems it is a lost cause they
are going to continue to tax and
spend this nation and our freedom out
of existence, that is a given.

But, you see, the GOP is also hell bent
on feeding this same beast, but,
trying to put it on a lesser spending
diet. The GOP I believe intends to
cut, manage, and try to make sense of
a burned out unworkable and
doomed system. Which, I'm sure in
actuality will speed up the demise
of the whole system.

Directly or indirectly the profit from
private business and mostly small
businesses is the sole support that
keeps government operating. And
for a long time now that support has
not been able to keep our welfare
state beast fed. So, higher taxes will
mean even less profit from small
business for government to tax.

Now, if the GOP starts cutting and
slashing we will end up with a
smaller pie that must feed the same
amount of needy greedy dependent
mouths. No one believes in
independency and self-sufficiency more
than I do, but, I think it is cruel to kick
a crutch from under anyone unless
they have some type of lifeline to hold

on to.

Like a broken record here I go again
on what I think must be done for this
nation to survive. First, rip the
minimum wage up by the root and
eliminate it entirely, then burn it where
it can't come back. Next, to give
the poor, the disadvantage, and elderly
a lifeline, the government should
establish government run
commissaries, housing, and clinics.

Also, the government should issue
tokens or script to all who qualify for
these services to keep from causing
inflation in the free market national
currency. Next, the government must
never give anyone free unearned
money but still pay hard currency to
those that work for the
government.

Doing it this way will stop
contaminating the national free market
currency and will stop driving the cost
of living out of sight for everyone. And
lastly, government ought to void all
taxes except on physical property and

then only enough for national defense, interior, and the operation of government.

Hell, I know this is extreme but do we really have a choice? Because A total collapse is coming anyway and the most we can do is try to survive and live through it, mother natures bust cycle will not be denied. But, at least this way if we act first we should be able to survive with our freedom still in tact.

I know my advice will be ignored but at least it will give wise men something to think about, "A word to the wise is sufficiency."
SIRMANS LOG: 7 OCTOBER 2012, 1252 HOURS

HOW TO SAVE USA AND GLOBAL ECONOMY: "GOOD GOVERNMENT IS A PROTECTOR NOT A PROVIDER!"

MY ANALYSIS ON ROUND 1 OF THE 2012
PRESIDENTIAL DEBATE SERIES.

Let me, Freddie L. Sirmans, Sr. the great self-made writer weigh in. It was not even close in my opinion, Mitt won by a country mile. But, I doubt the polls will move very much in his favor.

Folks, I'm a writer and I'm not running for anything now or ever, so that leaves me free to shoot from the hip and many times I'm wrong, but even a stopped clock is right twice a day.

The reason why I don't think the polls will move very much in Mitt's favor is because we live in a welfare state which means we have masses upon masses of government's dependents that believe in big government heart, body and soul.

And their one and only focus and interest are "What has government done for me lately." These dependents are bonded to the Democratic Party like a child is bonded to its mother.

That means these dependents will

never be swayed with reason and logic, some where along the line an indelible stamp was put on their brain that the republicans is the enemy. And the only thing that can remove that stamp is to become an independent thinker.

However, no dependent thinker volunteers to become an independent thinker they must be forced to fend for themselves to become an independent thinker. All of that means these big government dependents are going to emotional support and vote democratic no matter how their candidate performs.

That is why I think it is short sighted to chase after people who will never vote republican under no condition, instead I think they should be pounding and pounding to no end lower taxes across the board, more jobs, and strong national defense with no regret, anything else create class envy.

It is very simple, if the republicans can't win with lower taxes "The

inmates has already taken over the
asylum" anyway. So, in the grand
scheme of things, my final analysis is
what do it really matter who win
the election anyway both candidates is
determine to save the welfare
state.

In my view the welfare state is over
done for and need to be buried, I
think it is impossible for the USA and
western civilization to survive
unless the welfare state is abandon,
period. Also, I think anyone that
thinks the welfare state can be saved
can't possible understand the free
market or economics, period.

I may be wrong about a lot of things
but without a doubt in my mind I
know the welfare state can't possible
be saved. With the damaged it
has done to western civilization we will
be lucky if we survive at all
without going back to the Stone Age
even if we abandon it today.

Otherwise mother nature is on the
brink of stepping in herself, and I

will tell you now if we don't act now a
totally economic collapse is going
to happy any day now. Unless my
super natural wisdom advice is
heeded western civilization is doomed
anyway in my view.

Yes, little old me has the answer.
Again here is my survival solution, first
get rid of the minimum wage entirely,
rip it out by the root. Next, establish
government run commissaries,
housing, and clinics and use tokens or
script for the poor, disadvantage,
elderly, or whoever qualifies for aid.

Third void all taxes except enough
property tax for national defense,
interior, and the operation of
government, because it is going to
come to that anyway when this
economy soon totally collapse.

Forth, Government get the hell out of
the free market, stay with collecting
the taxes due, protecting and
defending the country, and then the
American people will save themselves
and the government, too. But, to

continue with this nanny state we have
no chance of continuing to survive,
period.

Hell, I know I'm not going to be taken
serious, but, I'm a writer and I
writer what I think, I can't make
anyone believe or act upon anything I
write, but, believe it or not at least it is
food for though. And while I'm
at it, another thing, everyone thinks
the boom and bust cycle is a bad
thing, wrong.

The boom and bust cycle is a law of
nature, and at some point the cycle
must be completed. I believe time has
finally ran out and the bust cycle
is answering the call of nature and no
matter what man does the bust
cycle is going to complete its rotation.

I think nothing man does is going to
stop it; I think all we can do is
prepare to survive it. There are certain
things throughout history that
only Mother Nature's purges solved.
Just look around at the USA, the
anti-survival negative forces has just

grown too powerful and only
Mother Nature can bring them back
under control.

Just look at the moral decay, the lack
of family values, the murdering of
the innocent unborn in the womb and
on and on. When all of these
negative anti-survival forces like men
marring men and women marring
women and all the rest becomes the
norm a country is ripe to be taken
over, there is no way in hell it can
survive long term.

So, if man can't or won't deal with the
situation, natures purges are
sure to reset the clock. It has been
proven in over 6,000 years of
written history that the only way man
can survive these purges of nature is
with a strong nuclear and extended
family system, a strong religious and
moral code, and adequate emergency
bartering capacity with many small
farmers and home gardeners.

Without these survival systems in
place no civilization has ever been

known to survive. Because of the "New deal" which birthed the welfare state, we have almost none of these survival systems left to survive nature's bust purge which is now coming upon us.

Our only hope is to act now before it fully hit, then it may be too late for the world. Lord, have mercy on the USA.
SIRMANS LOG: 4 OCTOBER 2012, 1327 HOURS

I CAN'T POUND IT ENOUGH, THE MINIMUM WAGE MUST GO!
OK, lately I have kept up this constant drum beat to eliminate the minimum wage. There is a deep reason for that, that doesn't meet the eye of those with little depth and perspective. To me the minimum wage roots grow far deeper than wages and what one earns.

To me the minimum wage is the foundation and corner stone of the welfare state. If the minimum wage

was eliminated nation wide it
would be the first step back to a true
free market place economy. And if
that was followed up by separating
government spending from the
national economy a miracle would take
place.

The problem with the USA economy is
it is being used like in an incest
relationship and is feeding on it's self.
You See the government itself is what
driving up consumer inflation out of
sight. The government is taking tax
payers money and giving it free
unearned to the poor and thereby
driving up the cost of living on the tax
payers and everyone.

Food stamps and unearned money
given to some citizens by the
government flood what little left of a
free market we have and
contaminates it by providing a big
enough pool of payers to prevent any
reduction in prices.

Sure, I feel as a last resort the
government must help the poor and

disadvantage. But, the only way the government can help the poor and others without destroying the free market place is by establishing government run commissaries, housing, and clinics and using tokens or script for those that qualify.

Doing it this way will keep government spending separated and out the free market and prevent contamination by not driving up the cost of living on the tax payers. It is simple you can't have a true free market economy with a minimum wage.

There is this false assumption that booms and busts cycles are a bad thing. Sure, no one likes to loose money or go out of business, but cycles are a must for survival, period. It is a law of nature that everything must have a cycle to exist; there must be life and death to maintain life.

Life could not be maintain with life only or death only, with life only one thing would crowd out the universe. Man does have the ability to manipulate

and extend the economic cycle for
longer periods of time, but according
to the law of nature the cycle must be
completed sooner or later.

However, to extend the life of an
economy too long comes with a big
price, that price is it allows the anti-
survival and negative forces in life
to become more and more powerful.
There is no such a thing as
something all good or all bad.
Everything is relative in some way; too
much of a good thing is bad.

So, in an economy when you don't
allow small purges like business
failures which is the bust cycle to get
rid of and prevent the build up of
rot, moral decay, and inefficiency you
become an enabler to the growth
of anti-survival forces. And the longer
man puts off the bust cycles by
bailing out and propping up rot, decay,
and inefficiency the more
drastic action must be taken.

If nature's supreme law of natural
selection have to step in then it may

mean back to the Stone Age. Right now it is too late, the USA government will never save the economy from a total collapse, but I will tell you what will, take my advice in this article.

Start by first eliminating the minimum wage, next separate government spending from the free market national economy. To sum it up, eliminate the minimum wage and get as close as possible to a true free marker place, then the USA will survive with freedom intact.

Otherwise, the whole world may go back to the stone age. I am saying again, and again, and again, the minimum wage must go, not lowered, but ripped out by the root, or else. SIRMANS LOG: 26 SEPTEMBER 2012, 2351 HOURS

GOP AND DEMS HORSE RACE IN DEAD HEAT ROUNDING CURVE INTO FINAL STRETCH!
Ok, Ok, now they are approaching the final turn going into the home

stretch to win the big November 2012
USA presidential election sweep
stake. Folks, look like its going to be a
photo finish by a nose.

I, Freddie L. Sirmans, Sr. self-made
great writer will give a quick
analysis on winning or losing a race
like this. And at this stage it is still
too close to call, no one truly knows
who the winner will be. To be fair I
must say up front that I am bias
because of my conservative and in
many cases extreme views, I'm for
small government and low taxes.

Now, let me delve into the meat of the
subject, I think the only different
between the two horses is how fast we
loses our freedom after the
election. That is because to maintain
civil order we as a country must
eliminate the "Minimum wage" or turn
into a dictatorship or some other
form of authoritarian rule.

I believe within the next four years
they are going to finish selling off
the rest of USA sovereignty to support

the welfare state. And that is going to
cause mass uprisings that will lead to
martial law and finally dictatorship or
authoritarian rule. Wow! I'm getting
too far off track, let me get back to the
2012 horse race.

I believe if the Dems win we will lose
our freedom at a quick rapid fire
pace, whereas if the GOP win we will
lose it at a drip by drip pace, but,
at least the latter will allow more time
for a possible miracle to save our
freedom.

My take is the GOP has decided to run
their horse with a blank slate
strategy and use an attack and drive
up the other horse's dislike-ability.
I think it is an insane strategy, but,
who knows it may really work. I
think they figure the liberal media
won't have a big target to shoot at
and they can drive up the Dems
horse's dislike-ability enough to pull of
at least a narrow victory.

Who knows they may be right.
However, overall I beg the difference;

I think that strategy is just too risky. Sure, a lot of voter may vote for you because they hates the other horse more, but in most cases that is just not going to be enough.

So, the main flaw I see in that strategy is it is just too risky in my view, plus, I see another reason why that is unlikely to work. In my view when dealing with Dems and liberals you are not dealing with reasonable and rational beings in terms of long term USA survival. They want their government goodies now, to hell with y'all and long term survival of the whole nation.

Sure, they are good and decent Americans and I love them dearly. But, after years and years of socialist/liberal media indoctrination true reality has yet to set in. There are millions upon millions that believe government help will always be there to aid them not realizing that there has never been and never will be a government that didn't go broke at some point.

And I give this government four years at most, but, of course I pray that I'm wrong. Back to the horse race, Even if the GOP did succeed in their strategy, which they won't because the liberal media will never allow it.

But, even if they did brand the Dems horse as a terrible socialist, all would happen is the masses of government dependents would say he is our socialist and we know he will protect and take care of us, and prove it with their vote. That is the facts and why I think the bland strategy is severely flawed.

I am only writing my views and opinions, no one really knows, the bland strategy could still hit pay dirt. My low taxes, more jobs, and strong national defense advocacy is risky too, especially in today's liberal hollering high tax climate. I'm one that believe in "No guts no glory," Take a stand you believe in and fight tooth and nails to defend it, some one has to lose.

The three things I have strongly advocated has long been proven guaranteed GOP winners, which is lower taxes, more jobs, and strong national defense. But, in my view the GOP no longer believe in them or doesn't have the gut to run on them, especially lower taxes, how sad.

Hell, if the GOP can't still win on lower taxes and more jobs, "The inmates has already taken over the asylum, anyway," but I don't believe that has actually happened, yet. Even if one loses, stand for your beliefs, freedom means standing for what you believe in.

Washington standing tall in the boat crossing the Delaware, everyone without a doubt knew what he was standing for. Agree or not that is my analysis of the November 2012 big presidential horse race fixing to go into the final stretch.

Like I've said before I am just a lone neurotic self-made writer with super natural God give wisdom, what

the hell do I know? So far no one
ever seems to pay any attention to a
damn thing I say, still, I enjoy
writing and expressing my views. I
dearly love this great country, the
only one I know.
SIRMANS LOG: 24 SEPTEMBER 2012,
1414 HOURS

THE MINIMUM WAGE IS STANDING IN
THE WAY OF USA SURVIVAL!
Right now the USA has more ability to
survive on it's own than any nation on
earth. In raw talent, ability, and
natural resources the USA is
unsurpassed.

The problem with the USA is it has
allowed the liberals and their welfare
state to get a deadly choke hold on the
nation neck and we are being
strangled to death. The ultra high
taxes and murdering regulations are
slowly killing this great nation. It is too
late now the USA government no
longer has the wisdom or the will to
save this great nation in my view.

The ever increasing high taxes and choking regulations will in a couple of years make it impossible for private business to make enough profit to survive. And the economically ignorant general public doesn't have a clue that all government funding originates from the profit of private business.

So, very soon our welfare state ain't gonna have the funds to save anyone, it is already flat broke and you can juggle the books and run schemes but only so long. As of now the people themselves are the only thing that can save the great USA.

They can still save the great USA by buying, selling, and maybe even bartering with each other to feed themselves and survive, after all people traded and bartered for thousands of years before money was invented.

In fact the American Indian survived for centuries and never had a currency. To survive sometimes you

gotta do what you gotta do. One
must have food, shelter, and warmth
to survive, then every thing else is
gravy when times get hard enough.

Going this route hopefully the
government can still tax enough to
maintain security if nothing else, at
this stage this is the wisest course to
take. Otherwise if we keep trying to
save the welfare state I guarantee you
we will end up with a dictator or some
form of
authoritarian rule, and if that happens
100 million starving to death will
be a low figure in my view.

There is no doubt in my mind if
allowed to the people will take the bull
by the horns and do whatever it take
to survive. The people can and will
save the great USA but there is a
problem, as it is they can't, even it
being the last chance and hope for USA
survival.

You see, the "Minimum wage is
standing right dab in the middle of the
way and if it is not ripped up by the

root and completely eliminated it is
over for the great USA, we will be
totally doomed. I have pounded and
pounded this fact to no end all to no
avail everyone seems to think I'm
crazy.

But, where there is a will there is
always a way and I still have hope.
So, as long as there is still breath in
my body I will be pounding for the
elimination of the minimum wage. Just
maybe enough people will wake
up before it is too late.

Thank you God for my life, health, and
strength, I am truly blessed and have
so much to live for, thank you, thank
you, thank you...
SIRMANS LOG: 14 SEPTEMBER 2012,
1905 HOURS

WELL, I GUESS I FINALLY LOST MY
COTTON PICKING MIND
I am only one man, a pitiful looking
little neurotic handicap armed only
with a pen going up against this
awesome almighty omnipotent welfare

state. It is just like the classic battle of
David going up against Goliath
armed only with a slingshot.

I think in about four years the
socialist/liberal news media is going to
be the most surprised of all. That is
because they are the first ones that
must go when a dictator or an
authoritarian government starts
consolidating power.

Like I've said before I believe the
economy is going to totally collapse
within four years. That being the case I
think the take over will start
with martial law, and then a dictator or
some type of authoritarian
regime will emerge.

The only thing that is going to save the
America economy from a totally
collapse is the complete elimination of
the minimum wage, period,
nothing else can save us. Mainly
because the welfare state have
destroyed any backup or safely valve
to survive on like a strong nuclear
and extended family system.

The things that allowed civilization to
survive for over 5,000 years like a
strong nuclear and extended family
system, strong moral and family
values, and adequate emergency
backup bartering capacity with many,
many small farmers and home
gardeners are all almost nonexistent.

We have almost no means of surviving
when the economy totally
collapses. And that is a fact that the
liberals are too shallow to ever see
until people starts starving by the
millions. It is completely get rid of
the minimum wage or back to the
Stone Age, there is no other option.

I'm no fool I know today's politicians
will never totally eliminate the
minimum wage, still, I must never stop
pounding and pounding away
because it is my destiny and duty to
keep sounding the distress call,
come hell or high waters. God save
America.
SIRMANS LOG: 12 SEPTEMBER 2012,
2049 HOURS

AGAIN, THE MINIMUM wage MUST BE
RIPPED UP BY THE ROOT AND
COMPLETELY ELIMINATED.
I know a lot of people don't understand
my thinking and writing, but, I'm not
just out here free wheeling it there is a
method to my insanity or wisdom that
guides me.

So, let me shine some light on what
guides me. The reason I know
without a shadow of a doubt that I am
right and in time will be vindicated is
because my thinking is in line with
nature's supreme law of "Natural
selection."

A society must have government for
the protection of the whole society,
but, pertaining to the economy
government involvement and force is
the worst thing you can have. That is
because force flies into the face of
nature's supreme law of "Natural
selection."

The law of "Natural selection" is what

controls everything and all existence, and it is based on a survival need. If there is no survival need for it, any and everything starts ceasing to exist. The old saying is really true, "If you don't use it you lose it."

So, when government forces a "Minimum wage" on the people the ability to hire people at any cost starts ceasing to exist. Even a giant mighty oak tree didn't start big but instead started from a wee little acorn.

The "Minimum wage" must be ripped up by the root and completely eliminated if the USA and western civilization is to have any chance of survival. Otherwise, according to nature's supreme law of "Natural selection" it will be impossible for the USA to survive as 57 states, every special interest group and faction in the nation will soon be at each others throat.

There will be no way of avoiding it, back to the Stone Age will be our

destination. I know that around 99.9
percent of the American people
think I'm insane for wanting to
completely get rid of the minimum
wage, still that don't prove me wrong.

God has blessed me with this great
super natural wisdom for a reason.
No matter how handicapped or
seemingly unqualified I may be the
distress call must be sounded and go
forth regardless, it is my destiny
and it is bigger than my well being or
survival.

This whole thing is like the classic
battle of good versus evil. There are
some who think my way of thinking
represents evil by wanting to set
things back to when many didn't have
certain rights. But, I'm not about
taking away anyone's rights I am
strictly against anything of the sort.

What I am about is saving human
beings and many of the old values is
what allowed civilization to survive for
over 5,000 years. The nuclear
family, good moral values, and

adequate bartering capacity are a
must, and without them no society can
survive for very long, period.

Today in the USA every one of those
three values is in almost total ruins. I
have no bitterness towards anyone; I
know I can see much more than the
average person in term of survival.

An example is like many people that
have been severely injured or had
something bad happen to them, but
later said they was glad it
happened because it opened their
eyes, and they can now see things
that was always right before their
eyes.
SIRMANS LOG: 8 SEPTEMBER 2012,
1026 HOURS

CAN GENERAL MOTORS WITHSTAND
THE TEST OF TIME?
Folks, I try to leave certain things
alone, but I just couldn't hold my
tongue any longer or I was going to
pop if I didn't vent. What I am
talking about is all of this bragging by

the shallow minded liberals about saving general motors.

Well, I for one have a different opinion about that matter. In my view liberals just simply doesn't have the depth to understand democracy or the free market, period. Our liberal created welfare state is what has created all these shallow minded liberals that are coming out of the woodworks armed with unsound judgment.

The liberals have not saved general motors what they really have done is made it another big government dependent. The very basics of understanding life, growth, and survival, or just existence itself are to know that you have to get rid of rot, decay, and inefficiency.

You just simply can't have progress, growth, and long term success without allowing failure. What government has actually done to general motors is create another burden on the American tax payers.

And from now on it will always be a burden because its management will never make the hard decisions to get rid of enough rot, decay, and inefficiency to become totally independent and profitable.

Sure, it is propped up now, but this government is broke and will soon be going under, then what? This nation has bankruptcy laws which mean general motors would have survived, but leaner and meaner, I think saving the unions and keeping liberal voters happy definitely was a factor. But, instead we have a wobbly kneed colossal big government dependent for life.

In closing, I'm just one self-made neurotic writer with an opinion, what the hell do I know?
SIRMANS LOG: 6 SEPTEMBER 2012, 2337 HOURS

WHAT DO AFRICANS AMERICANS AND WOMEN HAVE IN COMMON?
What do African Americans and women

have in common; they both have a
very high dependency mentality. This
is not intended to put these two
demographics down in any way; this is
to try to understand the why of this
phenomenon.

Plus, I don't think this is necessarily a
bad thing, it allowed African
Americans as a race to survive in a
hostile environment right out of
slavery. But, this is a new day and it is
time for African Americans as a
race to think as individuals and be
more responsible for their own
survival.

When are Africans Americans on a
wide scale going to provide more of
their own businesses to provide jobs
and do more of the hiring of their
own people, cry me a river? I am
retired now, but over the years I have
hired people and provided jobs.

On a mass scale what the hell survival
need can a poor black man offer
a woman when uncle sugar is her
Great white father provider, you tell

me. To act responsible there must be a survival need to be responsible according to nature's supreme law of "Natural selection."

The welfare state has just about taken all responsibility away from the poor black man in the African American community, and the rest of the nation will soon follow suit. So, how can you expect someone to be responsible when they have never been conditioned to be responsible, you can't logically? I totally blame the shallow minded liberals for this situation.

As a writer I am only trying to get at the facts and wade through all of the myths and emotionalism. I'm one that believes that almost nothing about life is innate; it is all learned in some way. I believe a new born baby's brain starts off as a clean slate.

So, there must be a logical reason why 90 percent plus African Americans as a group always vote for one political party. It is like the unbreakable bond between a mother and child. In my books and writings I go deep into the reasons why African Americans think the way they do.

But, for now I will move on to the political reality of dealing with the said two demographics groups. If conservatives and republicans are thinking about winning these two groups over with reason, forget it, it ain't gonna happen. There is an emotional bond here with the Democratic Party that can't be broken with no amount of reasoning.

These two groups see the Democratic Party like a child sees its parents. It is all about dependency versus independency. Dependency is the nesting syndrome, and the only way to break the nesting syndrome is to kick the dependent out of the nest, that is what the
mother eagle does.

But, for African Americans, mentally we are still in the nest and will stay there as long as we have a welfare state. And the really sad part is the welfare state has almost totally destroyed the African American culture and nuclear family and is fast working on the entire nation.

And another thing, the poverty pimps are making sure that African Americans never leave the safety of the nest. They guarantee that African Americans won't ever be able to jettison their dependency slave mentality.

African Americans still mentally see the master's beer as colder and if given a choice won't automatically support his look alike brothers and sisters in business or otherwise.

The African American elite won't create zones in and around an all African American neighborhood to live but instead get as far away as they can afford.

Sure, the excuse now is crime is the big problem but I don't buy that for one second as the only reason,

because the movie "A raising in the
sun" showed escaping from black
neighborhoods long before the welfare
state kicked the black man out of the
home to create all of this crime.

I see a culture problem here, but the
poverty pimps are still fighting
both tooth and nails to keep African
Americans in the nest as helpless
victims, instead of taking more
responsibility for our own survival
come
hell of high waters.

As a race we owned and controlled far
more before the welfare state came
along and destroyed the black
community. My God what a sad
situation, still, I wish all people
goodwill including the good intention
poverty pimps.

It is the welfare state that has created
all of these dependents and if
they haven't reached a majority yet it
is only a matter of time before
they do and send us all back to the
Stone Age.

I think we still have a majority in hard working tax payers and independents that will give conservatives and republicans a political Trifecta in November but just barely, on one condition.

That one condition is the republicans must pound and pound to no end low taxes, more jobs, and strong national defense. Otherwise, Lord knows I hope I'm wrong, but I just don't believe the republicans can win it otherwise.

Myself, I am a conservative at heart but in practice I'm a realist.
SIRMANS LOG: 31 AUGUST 2012, 1303 HOURS

CURRENT EVENTS: WHY CRUCIFY ONE FOR A BAD CHOICE OF WORDS?
This abortion flap going around that is supposed to be so outrageous is only a modern thing. Until within the last one hundred years an unborn child conceived through rape was

almost never killed.

In fact some believe that the child
itself acts as a healing process from a
horrible traumatic event. Back then the
racial element was the only thing that
guaranteed the killing of the unborn
child of the rape victim in some cases.

So, in my opinion why should a poor
choice of words create all of this
ado about something the moral
bankrupted liberals would like to
exploit? And all liberals are not
democrats. This is the sort of thing
that
can end up biting the self-righteous.

What is freedom if a man can't defend
the unborn, we have no future if
no one defends the unborn. It's no
wonder social security is going
under we have killed off a whole
generation of payers.
SIRMANS LOG: 21 AUGUST 2012,
0150 HOURS

FAR TOO MANY AMERICANS ARE JUST

PLAIN ECONOMICALLY IGNORANT!
Economically speaking "What belongs
to everyone belongs to no one," in
theory, maybe not, but, in actually
practice it's definitely true.

Okay, this idea that the government
did it, that the roads, bridges, and
infrastructure provided the means or
the individual couldn't have done
it is shallow negative thinking in my
view, but many liberals think that
way.

That type of thinking places the cart
before the horse. Government is a
necessary parasite that every society
must have to provide internal and
external protection. In a free society
government can't sustain itself or
produce a profit, it survives only on
what it takes in the form of profit
from what always originates from
some form of private business
transaction, period.

Sure, the government got the roads,
bridges, and infrastructure, but,
where the hell you think government

got the seized money from to do
that? Not that I disagree, but it got the
money out of the profit of many,
many struggling small businesses.

All of this anti-business propaganda is
just plain economic ignorance. They
have no idea what made America the
greatest and wealthiest nation in the
history of mankind.

Without the millions upon millions of
small private businesses out there
making a profit there will be no profit
for the government to take to
provide anything for anyone, period.

Lord have mercy on our great nation,
with all of this negative anti-business
propaganda thinking out there we are
going to need it.
SIRMANS LOG: 20 AUGUST 2012,
1201 HOURS

IF THE REPUBLICAN DOESN'T WIN A
POLITICAL TRIFECTA IN NOVEMBER IT
WILL BE THEIR OWN FAULT!
I have pounded it to where I am

almost blue in the face; conservatives
limit your message to around three
things. Sure, you respond to any and
everything then its I stand by my
earlier statement.

I know staying with so few things will
bore the hell out of most people but
that is what you want, that is proof
they are not forgetting what you
stand for.

The simple minded and many others
will succumb to the course of least
resistance and grab the democrat
goodies that is why the default volt
almost always goes to the democrats.
And unless a conservative stand
for lower taxes, more jobs, and strong
national defense the default volt
will carry the day in the general
election most of the time.

In my view the problem with the
republicans is they are out there
attacking for blood and is acting and
reacting all over the map and no
one truly knows what they stand for.
To hell with the other guy, the people

want to know what about you, what
are you gonna do, can I trust and
depend on you.

The hard working independents and
majority tax paying voters will
never desert one who pounds to no
end lower taxes, more jobs, and
strong national defense. Yet,
somewhere in the polling it got
republicans running away from the
three things I advocate especially
lower taxes.

I say to hell with all of this polling go
with your gut sometime, people
want someone who is willing to go
down with what they themselves
believe in and what is right for
America.

I will tell you now if you are afraid to
pound away on lower taxes your
chance of winning in November are
going to be slim to none and that is
nobodies fault but your own.
SIRMANS LOG: 14 AUGUST 2012,
0852 HOURS

THE REPUBLICANS WILL WIN IN NOVEMBER 2012, BUT, I BELIEVE THEY TOO WILL FAIL, TOO!

Well, we now know who the republican vice presidential candidate will be and my prediction was wrong. Obviously there is going to be a new team after November 2012, but, in my view the republicans will at least buy a little more time before the USA and world economy collapses. Otherwise, to keep the same team we go dictatorship or some other authoritarian rule right away because I believe the economy will totally collapse within three years.

The sad fact is THE WELFARE STATE can't be saved and anyone that thinks it can is in denial. I can dissect an economy as well as anyone and I'm telling you the days of the welfare state is over we are now living on borrowed time.

The republicans just as the democrats are dead set on saving the welfare state but I'm telling you the republicans will fail even worse

than the dems simply because they
think they can cut the growth of
government, wrong.

It is impossible to reduce the growth of
government in this welfare state
because there are too many social
programs that will kick in and
increase the dole side of government,
thereby growing government in a
reverse negative way. There is no need
to add more details they can be
found farther down in my writing.

All I will say at this time is we must
start somewhere to prevent going
back to the Stone Age. The first thing
that must be done or nothing else
matters anyway because holding on to
the welfare state leads only back
to the Stone Age.

The complete elimination of the
minimum wage must be done now or it
will be impossible for the USA
government to survive, that is a fact,
there is not a doubt in my super mind
about that. You don't have to
believe me just keep on living; the

minimum wage must go, one way or another if we are to have any chance of survival as a nation.

I pound and pound this fact and still no one wants to hear it but we all will sooner than we think. The elimination of the minimum wage will allow the American people to save themselves because soon the government is not going to have the money to do so.

The government doesn't generate any profit it is a necessary parasite and every penny it takes in comes from some form of private business profit. And in this anti-business atmosphere the shallow minded liberals are trying to make it impossible for a business to make a profit.

The liberal and masses of economically ignorant government dependents are biting the hand that feed them and the really sad part is they don't have a clue absent the bias predominant socialist/liberal news media. God I ask in your name, save the only home I know.

SIRMANS LOG: 12 AUGUST 2012,
0203 HOURS
PS: All solutions on how to save the
USA economy and western
civilization can be found farther down
in my writing.

WHO WILL BE THE 2012 REPUBLICAN
VICE PRESIDENTIAL CANDIDATE?
Only the republican presidential
candidate himself, his wife, and just
maybe a very few trusted confidants
knows. Still, that doesn't stop
almost everyone from the political
experts to the man on the streets
from guessing who it will be. I decided
to join the crowd and participate
in the guessing game.

With nothing more to go on but my
own gut feelings I'm taking a shot in
the dark and predicting the republican
vice presidential candidate will be Rick
Santorum. There will be no surprises
there; I think the governor
is a very, very cautious man.
SIRMANS LOG: 5 AUGUST 2012, 0928
HOURS

ARE REPUBLICANS AFRAID TO
PROMOTE LOWER TAXES?
Folks, I am a self-made writer and a
screwed up neurotic one at that.
But, one thing I am not is a phony
hypocrite. I may not be a man of
extra strong physical courage and feel
overall I am too passive. Still, I
think I am a man of conviction and I
try to do my best in spite of my
handicaps.

I said all of that to try to make a point,
it is no wonder the survival of our
freedom is under attack. I feel we may
lose our freedom because fewer and
fewer people are willing to standby
their true convictions. Every politician
seems to be putting a finger up into
the wind by means
of political polling.

The republicans had a TRIFECTA in the
bag, but, I feel they stand a
good chance of losing now simply
because they are too afraid to stand
up to their convictions. Instead they

are putting all of their faith in all of
this extreme polling; I hope they are
right for the sake of the country
and our freedom.

I really don't have a favorite political
party my only concern is who will
best hold on to our dwindling supply of
freedom. Even if the republicans
do win the TRIFECTA it will only allow a
little more time before nature's
supreme law of "Natural selection"
lowers the boom.

The republicans don't need to give out
a lot of details all they need to do
is just pound and pound to no end
lower taxes, more jobs, and strong
national defense and nothing else. But,
I believe they are afraid to pound
lower taxes, and what I say to that is
when the majority of Americans don't
want lower taxes the country is no long
worth saving anyway.

If that is the case there soon won't be
any freedom left to save. We will
be a bankrupted welfare state headed
back to the Stone Age. No matter

what our beliefs are we all are Americans, you don't have to agree with anything I write, but thank God I still have the freedom to say the things I write.
SIRMANS LOG: 30 JULY 2012, 1219 HOURS

IS THE PENN STATE SLATE WIPED CLEAN ENOUGH?

As a writer with extreme perspective and supernatural wisdom sometimes I feel a need to stop in my tracks and just vent. As I look at world civilization and see where it is today I believe idominant western civilization that lead us here.

But, ever since the "New deal" and the birth of the welfare state we have lost our way. I know the great scholars and thinkers have come up with all kinds of reasons of the why of the decline.

But, as a creative super deep original thinker I have zeroed in on the lack of teaching the Christian faith as a big factor. And to focus in on even a

more precise point which is our loss of
the Power of forgiveness. Culture wise
it is a fact that un-forgiveness stops
growth and progress in its track and a
slow primitive regression backward
begins.

Sure, there is an exception to every
thing in life but as a rule the most
caring and forgiving people are those
that have faced the most
hardships and struggles. The Penn
State case prompted me to write this
article. All I ask is where does
individual accountability end?

No one can control what another
person may do. Do we really want to
go all the way back to the seventh
generation like in the Old Testament
to make sure the slate is clean? It may
come to that insanity.
SIRMANS LOG: 23 JULY 2012, 1229
HOURS

A CONSERVATIVE WILL ALMOST
ALWAYS LOSE THE GENERAL
ELECTION BY CONSTANTLY

ONLY ABOLISHING THE MINIMUM WAGE LAW CAN SAVE
THE USA NOW

ATTACKING!
Unless one has deep wisdom and
perspective they won't understand
why I'm so against all of this attacking.
It is simply because it is a
loser's strategy.

Today's voter has a short attention
span and need to be constantly
reminded of who you are and what you
stand for. Sure, attacking the
other guy tears him down, but that
doesn't remind quick forgetting
independents and the majority what
you stand for.

Everyone already knows the sugar
daddy/momma liberal is going to tax
and spend and give away the store
even when we can't afford it,
especially women and African
Americans already know this, they just
don't care.

It is like the warnings on a pack of
cigarettes and all of the warnings
against big juicy high fat burgers, etc.
people already know the danger
and choose high risk living, so

preaching fire and brimstone on how
bad
someone or something is may work
against a conservative but very
little against a sugar daddy liberal
giving out goodies. As long as the
goodies keep coming they will say "I
don't care if the canidate looks like
ET as long he is nice to me."

Knowing better we all has a weakness
to take the course of lease resistance
and grab the goodies, but if a mature
conservative step up and promise
lower taxes, more jobs, and strong
national defense he will win with the
independents and majority tax paying
public.

I'm telling you, in the general election
you don't normally beat a liberal
by constantly attacking, Reagan didn't
go that route nor did "W." Attacking in
itself distracts from who you are and
what you stand for, and in the final
analysis that is the reason people vote,
the individual
sometimes has little to do with it.

I would but there is no way in hell 90
percent plus African Americans
would vote for Herman Cain. He would
be the best friend we ever had
but there is an indelible stamp on too
many out there that says his way
of thinking is the enemy. Sure, some
people will vote for you simply
because they hate the other guy so
much, but in most cases it is going
to take a lot more than that to win.

So, those are the facts, it is what it is.
It is what you are going to do that
really matters and if conservatives are
not going to stress lower taxes, more
jobs, and strong national defense I
don't believe we will get the trifecta in
November. I certainly hope I'm wrong
on this.
SIRMANS LOG: 18 JULY 2012, 1440
HOURS

"NEVER LET THEM SEE YOU SWEAT"
Conservatives stay the course, stay the
course the socialist/liberal
news media shark feeding frenzy is a
sign of desperation to try to break

your pounding grip of low taxes, more
jobs, and strong national defense
only for the guaranteed TRIFECTA win
in November.

If you let them break your death grip
now we lose the TRIFECTA win it's
just that simple. People got eyes and
ears and independents and the
majority will never vote against one
that relentlessly pounds low taxes,
more jobs, and strong national defense
only unless the socialist/liberal
news media breaks your death grip.

Just keep pounding those three
priorities to no end because that is
your
armor and no minds will change,
except around forty percent who will
never vote for a conservative anyway.
"Never let them see you sweat"
just keep pounding; pounding and
pounding, freedom in America
depends on it.

They are going to throw everything at
you including the kitchen sink if
you are a conservative or have any

conservative's leanings, but just
keep pounding the said priorities and
they will never turn the
independents against you.
SIRMANS LOG: 17 JULY 2012, 2101
HOURS

IT'S OVER FOLKS; I DON'T SEE
ANYTHING BREAKING THE DEATH
GRIP CONSERVATIVES HOLD.
It is just a matter of time before all of
the flailing has to peter out. Unless the
pit bull like ceaseless pounding of low
taxes, more jobs, and strong national
defense eases up it is definitely over.

However, conservatives never ease up
or take anything for granted because it
in never official over until the last vote
is counted. The TRIFECTA super prize
win is unofficial now a done deal, hurry
up 3 November.

Let them flail away and holler all they
want to because nothing short of
easing up on the low taxes, more jobs,
and strong national defense
pounding can deny conservatives the

big TRIFECTA in November.
SIRMANS LOG: 15 JULY 2012, 1538
HOURS

CONSERVATIVES NOW HAVE A DEATH
GRIP ON A BIG TRIFECTA WIN IN
NOVEMBER!
I'm hearing people say attack back,
which is the normal thing to do, but
that is what the attack dog
socialist/liberal news media want you
to do
so you will then be in their brier patch
and people will forget what the
hell you stand for, and then they can
rip you apart with a thousand cuts.

I say to the conservatives you now
have the death grip just hold on like
a pit bull by keep pounding nonstop
low taxes, more jobs, and strong
national defense. You see the proof
that it is working by them flailing
away with all kinds of lies and
extremes like crazy trying to break
your
death grip on the TRIFECTA win in
November.

Their insane flailing is only preaching
to their own choir, the independents
and majority will never abandon one
who pounds endlessly low taxes, more
jobs, and strong national defense.
Discipline,
discipline, no matter what, just keep
pounding the said priorities and get the
TRIFECTA win in November. Glory be
to God.
SIRMANS LOG: 13 JULY 2012, 2250
HOURS

I BELIEVE CONSERVATIVES HAS A
SLIM TO NONE CHANCE OF WINNING
THE BIG TRIFECTA IN NOVEMBER
WITHOUT ADHERING TO MY ADVICE!
This is my advice to all conservatives
or anyone with conservatives leaning;
never stray from only three things, low
taxes, more jobs, and strong national
defense.

Sure, make just one statement on
current events or what ever but then
revert back to the three said priorities,
period. The attack dog predominate

socialist/liberal news media don't like
you and is going to do everything in
their power to defeat you. That said,
as a rule the general public tends to be
simple minded with short memories.

That means to win the big TRIFECTA
conservatives must keep it simple
with not more than the three priorities,
low taxes, more jobs, and strong
national defense only. Sure, doing that
will bore the hell out of most people,
but that is what you want up until the
election that will be proof that they
won't forget what you stand for.

Otherwise, off to the side stirring up
controversial and everything else
the independents and others attention
span won't remember what the
hell you stand for, then the liberal
news media will rip you apart. No
matter what the liberal news media
propaganda attack machine says
the independents and winning majority
will remain faithful and loyal if
you never depart from the three said
priorities, they are your armor.

I'm telling every conservative or anyone with conservative leaning if you don't take my advice we have a slim to none chance of winning the big TRIFECTA in November. That is just the way it is. There are no absolute guarantees in life the most anyone can do is create the best conditions to win.

The liberal news media propaganda attack machine in my view is the biggest obstacle standing between a big TRIFECTA conservative win for the conservatives in November. All they know is to attack, attack, and attack, and it is futile to try to defend against their every barrage without armor.

The three said priorities is your armor only if you bore the hell out of people by sticking only with them. Sticking with them conservatives win, veering off them then the liberal news media propaganda attack machine will rip you apart and defeat you.

God I ask in your name save our great

nation.
SIRMANS LOG: 12 JULY 2012, 1227
HOURS

WHAT IS IT ABOUT THE MINIMUM
WAGE THAT PEOPLE CAN'T
UNDERSTAND?
Cutting the minimum wage is cold,
wrong and a mistake, doing that will
only aggravate and increase poor
people's misery. No one has ever read
or heard me encourage lowering the
minimum wage, if you thought you
did you weren't listening.

I have been drum beating it until I'm
almost blue in the face to "Get rid
of the minimum wage that is a world of
difference from lowering the
minimum wage. I am talking about
eliminating the minimum wage
entirely, period. That is the only things
that would bring back some
sanity to our economy, and is the only
thing that will save the USA with
freedom intact.

Otherwise, welfare states worldwide

will become dictatorships or some other form of authoritarian rule within five years just to keep order. What people that lack perspective and a basic understanding of economics fail to realize is it is not the amount of money that matters; it is the buying power that truly counts.

Eliminating the minimum wage for the whole nation would shift the economy into a natural balance where money would count for something, or there would be no way to prevent bartering. The minimum wage is what allowed the welfare state a foot in the door, now the welfare state beast rules the roost.

A free market place economy is bases on the fact that any one can pay as much or less as he sees fit for a job so long as no one is forced to accept it, or even pay the help with commodities if no force is applied. Sure, what I just said was to the extreme, but, I am all about survival, and with the condition the USA is in financial, nothing should be ruled out.

In my humble opinion the only thing stopping the USA from becoming a dictatorship right now is the second amendment. However, after November all of that could drastically change, I think the hidden priority agenda will be to use some type of UN treaty to trump the second amendment and override the second amendment once and for all. That is my analysis.

The liberals are just waiting on their chance to pounce. I ask in your name, God save freedom in America. SIRMANS LOG: 10 JULY 2012, 1447 HOURS

NEGATIVE ADS WORK, SURE, WITH IGNORANT AND UNINFORMED PEOPLE, BUT NOT WITH ME.
I'm one that has never bought into this idea that negative ads always work. Sure, they work with the ignorant and uninformed but not everyone fits that description.

I hold to the rule that if you are a good
and decent person and makes
sure people know what you stand for
then good and decent people will
support you. In politics I think the
dumbest thing one can do is exercise
in futility by trying to defend against
every bad or incorrect charge
directed against you. At worst even if
they brand you a SOB, what else
is new, like Nixon said, sure, he is a
SOB but he is our SOB.

As long as the conservatives keep
pounding low taxes, creating more
jobs, and strong national defense and
nothing else the independents
and vast majority won't care what the
bias socialist/liberal news media
propaganda attack machine brands
you. And they will prove it by
saying he is our SOB with their vote.

But, if the conservatives get side
tracked into shouting matches of he
said she said and every other kind of
juicy fodder it will be just what
the doctor ordered for the liberal
propaganda machine. Then with

phony polls and every other kind of
distortion one can imaging the
liberal propaganda attack machine will
rip you to threads and defeat you.
Staying with the three said things is
your armor, don't abandon them.
SIRMANS LOG: 4 JULY 2012, 1759
HOURS

GET OVER IT CONSERVATIVES
OBAMACARE IS NOW THE LAW OF THE
LAND AND THAT IS A FACT!
About this new Supreme Court ruling
on Obamacare, I think some
conservatives just ought to get over it,
period. They should realize what the
liberals have always known that the
constitution means only what
five people say it means.

From a political point of view you
control the court with the legislative
process by controlling who get on it,
not by ranting on and on over
spilled milk. Why do you think the die
hard liberals always fight to the last
man/woman over who gets on the
court, wake up and wise up

conservatives, it is all about control,
not ranting.
SIRMANS LOG: 4 JULY 2012, 1045
HOURS

A CONSERVATIVE ROYAL FLUSH WINNING HAND.
NEW INJECTION ADD-ON #2
In my view this whole Supreme Court
ruling is actually a God send to
conservatives. If conservative can't get
an overwhelming trifecta win
out of this they never will. With this
ruling conservatives is now holding
a royal flush sure winner going into the
November election.

However, the problem is the
conservatives don't know what to do
even if they do win the big trifecta
prize. The welfare state needs to be
dismantled and taken down but they
don't have the will or guts to take
on that issue.

The welfare state beast without a
doubt is going to soon collapse eating
us all one by one alive in the process,

so, where is the wisdom in failing
to take down this beast when you have
the power in your hands to do
so.

I doubt there will be any real changes
if the conservatives win big, I think
they will just try to feed the beast a lot
less by cutting back on everything,
which will end up even worse than
what the liberals did.

The reason why is we have a complete
welfare state and when you start
cutting back all that does is increase
the dole population, which is a no,
no. There is simply no way out except
using my "Any nation emergency
survival plan" which you will find
further down in my writing.
SIRMANS LOG: 2 JULY 2012, 2308
HOURS

NEW INJECTION: ADD-ON
In hind sight I think the court probably
did do the wisest thing. Otherwise the
whole liberal establishment would be
up in arms accusing the court of

someone who takes candy from a
baby.

To save freedom in America it is going
to take a miracle anyway, we are
too far gone. The liberal news media
propaganda machine has brain
washed far too many people, that the
government owes them a living.
I'm telling you there are no free rides
in nature, one way or another
someone always pays.

The liberal news media propaganda
machine has dumbed down the
population to the point now that the
dead beats and non-producer are
attacking the producers and the people
that makes this country work,
which is political suicide. "The inmates
are now beginning to take over
the asylum."

It is all starting to come to a head and
the election in November is only
how fast we lose our freedom. If the
democratic win the saving freedom
battle is totally lost and if the
republicans win it will only slow

the process down, but at least allow more time for a possible miracle.

Either way it is now time for Katie to bar the door. Forty percent are going to vote democratic no matter what and forty percent are going to vote republican no matter what, but, now I believe the lions share of the 20 percent independent swing vote is going republican because of Obamacare.

Freedom of the individual is on trial and without a miracle I don't see any hope of It surviving. I have thrown out a lifeline for the only way out but so far no one wants to take my bitter medicine. I have offered my bitter medicine throughout my writing many times before with no takers, but I will briefly outline it again.

Our welfare state provider government is the root problem; it has reached a tax raising saturation point and can't be saved. This is what must be done to save the USA and welfare states world wide to prevent them from becoming

dictatorships or some other form of
authoritarian rule.

With no exception the minimum wage
must be eliminated first and now,
not tomorrow or when we get around
to it. Next, government spending
must be separated from the free
market national economy now, not
later. This separation can only be done
by government establishing its
own commissaries, housing, and clinics
with the use of tokens or script.

This can be done almost overnight with
so many empty vacant building
in American cities. Excluding
government employees government
must never give anyone free unearned
money to spend in the national free
market economy that act alone is like
incest it pollutes and contaminates the
free market with consumer inflation.

It is like eating your seed corn or
drinking your priming water, that is
the main thing that has acted like a
cancer that have ate up welfare
states from the inside out worldwide.

Sure, government has a duty as a last resort to help the poor and disadvantage but never with cash handouts that will contaminate and destroy the national free market economy.

Government must operate it own commissaries, housing, and clinics with the use of tokens or script to keep it's spending separate and not destroy the national economy. There is no if's and's, or but's about it, if my solution is not accepted the welfare states worldwide will end up as dictatorships or some other form of authoritarian rule.

Freedom cannot and will not survive without most of its people disciplined with a sense of responsibility and accountability, period. The USA is almost there at the point of no return, far too many people thinks the government owes them a living with free Medicare. That is like asking doctors and health care workers to be slaves and give you free Medicare.

The welfare state has all but
completely destroyed our once strong
nuclear and extended family system,
our use to be strong religious and
moral way of life, and our former
adequate emergency backup bartering
capacity with many small farmers and
home gardeners, in
case the economy collapsed.

Now, we have nothing in terms of raw
survival when this bloated welfare
state collapses which could happen any
day now. When the USA and welfare
states world wide starts collapsing
which could
happen overnight and people get
hungry only an iron fist can maintain
order. And I'm not for sure even that
will save civilization from ending
back in the Stone Age.

Yet, they say I'm crazy and off my
rocker, so be it as long as I can
convince just one thick scull how dire
our situation is. I'll say it like this,
in the final analysis it is get rid of the
welfare states or accept our fate
and perish.

If we keep trying to save the welfare state nothing is going to save freedom and free enterprise, and I would bet my life on that if it would make a difference.
SIRMANS LOG: 1 JULY 2012, 1955 HOURS. NEW INJECTION END

I'm fixing to say something I shouldn't say and I don't know why I'm saying it but knowing me I'm going to say it anyway. I have said many times throughout my writing that "The Lord works in mysterious ways."

Well, no one disagrees more of what the Chief Justice did than me, it just doesn't make sense in my view. I have come to a conclusion that this is a case of divine intervention and a display of the power of destiny. Anyone with wisdom and perspective knows this is an earth shaking political game changer.

This is a conservative winning hand that even an idiot can't screw up.

Still, "Nothing is written in stone, and
never count your chicken before
they hatch."
SIRMANS LOG: 20 JUNE 2012, 2150
HOURS

CONFIRMING OBAMACARE MAY BE
THE STRAW THAT BROKE THE CAMELS
BACK!
WOW! OMG! Sold, sold, and sold by
the biggest bait and switch sale wrap-
up of the century. "My congrats to the
Lib's."

As one who loves freedom of the
individual I will be the first to disagree
with the Supreme Court confirming
OBAMACARE. However, why fret folks,
because in the grand scheme of things
the Supreme Court decision only
speeds up the demise of our welfare
state.

It is obvious the USA is going to go the
failed socialist course of Western
Europe, duh. In my view this is a sad
day for freedom loving Americans. To
make it simple where even an idiot can

understand, the days of the welfare
state are over, we are broke, no
money, can't pay, empty pockets,
what about no money people can't
seem understand, duh.

Financial wise the welfare state cannot
and will not survive, period. In a
way this confirming OBAMACARE may
be a blessing in disguise. The
working people who pay the bills and
make this country work may
finally wake up and vote in only
genuine conservative or face losing
this
great land of the free and home of the
brave.

Far too many people think the nation
owe them a living from years of
the liberal news media propaganda.
You can't get blood out of a turnip
simply because there is none there; it
is the same with OBAMACARE
there is no money there to pay for it
which is promoting false hope to
the people.

The USA government is already

borrowing forty cents of every dollar it
spends. And surely this
bigOBAMACARE add-on is going to be
the straw that broke the camel's back.
May God have mercy on the USA after
this
extreme lack of sound judgment by
people in high places?

God bless these leaders I'm sure they
did what they though what was
best for the country, it is not perfect,
still it is our system and I support
it one hundred percent without a
doubt. God bless America.
SIRMANS LOG: 28 JUNE 2012, 1208
HOURS

"We have a republic if we can keep it,"
that is truer today than it was over 200
years ago.

A BAD MARRIAGE!
I keep hearing market, market, and
market to no end, and I'm sick and
tired of it. That is the biggest problem
with the USA and welfare states

worldwide. The governments of local, state, and federal need to get the hell out of the stock market and the stock market need to get the hell out of the government.

They are two different things and don't mix. All government spending especially on an individual basis must be kept separated from the free market place economy, period, or else. SIRMANS LOG: 20 JUNE 2012, 2024 HOURS

A MOMENT OF THINKING OUT LOUD! I am paraphrasing, "There goes the dreamer, lets slay him and then see what happens to his dream. The waves of sin are a slow death to me." SIRMANS LOG: 18 JUNE 2012, 0013 HOURS

MY MINIMUM WAGE CRUSADE
One way or another the minimum wage is going to be completely eliminated. It boils down to how it gets done. At some point soon nature's

Supreme law of "Natural selection" is going to do it for the USA and all welfare states world wide unless we act first.

Ever since the "New deal" we have let the liberals call the tune and give away the store now we have to pay the piper in blood, sweat, and tears,
and even that may not be enough to save our nation.

There is no escaping our lack of judgment; it is a law of nature, there are no free rides. However, if the USA and the welfare states world wide go ahead and completely eliminate the minimum wage first modern civilization may be saved.

Otherwise, if nature's supreme law of "Natural selection" has to lower the boom then once the dominoes starts falling it may mean all the way back to the Stone Age. God, I ask in your name stay your hand!
SIRMANS LOG: 12 JUNE 2012, 1559 HOURS

SOME SOUL FOOD FOR THOUGHT
INJECTION, HERE.
Come on folks, I believe a new team
will be going in next year. "Big deal!
You are just one unknown self-made
writer with an opinion. Get lost."
However, I don't think I am alone on
thinking this, I think the
lib's want to change horses in
midstream but don't know how without
losing their 90 percent plus African
American monopoly vote forever.
But, find a way to blame it on the
republicans, problem solved.

Now, chew on that for a while. I'm a
creative writer folks, this is just food
for though and the wild imagination of
my deep, deep thinking. God save our
great nation.
SIRMANS LOG: 8 JUNE 2012, 1930
HOURS

"ANY NATION EMERGENCY SURVIVAL
PLAN" BY
FREDDIE L. SIRMANS, SR.
Folks, I am a self-made writer and I

tell it as I see it, straight raw no
chaser, right or wrong, believe it or
not, take it or leave it is what you get
from me.

Never mind the experts and learned
economist, I Freddie L. Sirmans, Sr.
with my great supernatural wisdom is
offering my "Any nation emergency
survival plan." Its coming folks, a
totally economic collapse,
and I am offering my plan free to
prevent total chaos that may lead
back to the Stone Age.

No, I haven't lost my mind I have been
writing basically the same thing for
over twenty years, now. Here is the
first thing that should be done now
even before nature's supreme law of
"Natural selection" lowers the
boom.

Any nation that expects to survive
when the boom is lowered and the
domino's starts falling best take heed
and act now because the whole
thing may be like a fast moving tree
top wild fire. Number one, the USA

and all of the welfare state must completely get rid of the "Minimum wage" now, not tomorrow or when you get around to it.

That would set free the free market place where it would function naturally like it is supposed to. Every business would still have to pay a higher wage to get the best workers.

But, free market means free without force, meaning if someone want to work for a dollar a day with room and board why shouldn't they have that right, because when this welfare state is flat broke and can't borrow another dine it may take something like that just to survive.

Number two, "All government free aid on an individual basis must be kept separated from the free market place national economy" because that is what causes consumer inflation and unreasonable prices. And the only way to keep free unearned government handout spending on an individual basis from subsiding price raising and contaminating the free market national economy is for government to use tokens or script and operate its own commissaries, housing, and clinics.

With unearned individual government spending being kept separate and not subsiding price raising no merchant can charge more than the poor and working class can afford because of their number, there is never enough rich to support an economy.

This way the poor and working class will be able to buy the bare necessities of food and medical care, and those that falls through the crack will get tokens or script as to not freeze or starve. This economic survival plan is not perfect but it is sound and will prevent total chaos.

The welfare state has spoiled a lot of people and following this plan won't be easy and will cause much hardship and pain, but, almost anything is better than losing our freedom forever or mired in total chaos.

With the minimum wage gone people will be free to barter or do whatever it takes to survive because a broke government may be lucky just to provide national defense, internally and externally.

This country has never known anything but freedom, and I assure you without the minimum wage blocking self-help the people will barter and do whatever it take to legally save themselves and the nation.
SIRMANS LOG: 27 MAY 2012, 0042 HOURS
PS: As always I don't expect my great supernatural wisdom to be taken seriously but positive human effort is never wasted.

HE/SHE IS OUR SOB!
One thing about Nixon is in private he was known for very colorful language. In one case one of his aides was branded on and on how bad he was. I'm paraphrasing Nixon's reply: "Sure, he is a SOB, but he is our SOB."

So, the message here to all
conservatives is: The socialist/liberal
news media propaganda attack
machine is definitely going to brand
from bottom to top anyone with any
conservative leaning a SOB.

But, the fact is as long as one keep
pounding until the cows come home
lower taxes, more jobs, and strong
national defense that will be their
armor plated protection.

Then no matter what they are labeled
or branded there will still be more than
enough freedom loving Americans to
carry the day, and say he is our SOB
with their vote.
SIRMANS LOG: 22 MAY 2012, 1222
HOURS

ADD ON INJECTION: 22 MAY 2012,
2118 HOURS
It is impossible to save a country or its
economy when its government
prevents big business failures. That
prevents any way to get rid of

waste, decay, and inefficiency. Doing that put's the whole country at risk by weighing down and crowding out positive new growth until a collapse is unavoidable.

Nature's supreme law of "Natural selection" doesn't hit any one on the head with a hammer, but nothing escapes it effect. "You can't get blood out of a turnip" for a simple reason, there is none there. It's the same with a broke government, soon its not going to take care of the elderly or anyone simply because there will be no money there.

The welfare state days are over and anyone disagreeing is simply economically ignorant and in a state of denial. Business profit is government's only means of support directly or indirectly, but by government promoting waste, decay, and inefficiency unabated soon it will be impossible for businesses to make a profit.

Knowing businesses can't make a profit

won't stop government from draining the last one dry. The reason is government sees itself as the great lord and master super social and family provider, plus the fear factor lets the politician know the masses will be coming with the pitch forks when no more government hand outs are forth coming.

Still, nothing is written in stone man still has the power to choose his destiny.

With all of these polls and figures flying around now-a-days I never forget, "Figures don't lie, but liars sure can figure."
ADD ON INJECTION END

WRITERS OPINION: LIBERALS ARE GOOD AND DECENT AMERICANS, TOO. Liberals are not bad people, almost all of my friends and relatives are liberals. In fact liberals in their minds mean well and have good intentions, but, the way to hell is paved with good intentions. Their problem as a rule is

they are just plain shallow and lack
perspective.
Liberalism is a modern phenomenon.

In the distance past just the day to day
struggle to survive made almost
everyone conservative. Back then you
had better instill accountability
and responsibility in your young if you
wanted any left because nature
and the elements were cruel, harsh,
and unforgiving.

There was no so called safety net. But,
in modern time especially with our
welfare state far too many people think
the world owes them a living. Far too
many people have what is called a
weak survival instinct due to a lack of
hardship and struggle.

I happen to believe that good
judgment and good character goes
hand
in hand. Many may disagree but I
believe that there must be at lease
some real or imposed hardship and
struggle to build good character. By
saying imposed that could mean

discipline or just taking away
privileges.

If one has a weak survive instinct I
just don't think they are equipped with
the judgment to safe guard and
protect future generations. No wonder
they are murdering future children in
the womb by the millions.

The lack of enough people with good
sound strong judgment in my view
is sealing our fate; after all you can't
get blood out of a turnip.

Before the "New deal" and the welfare
state it was mostly the rich that were
morally bankrupt, very few of the poor
believed in and aborted unborn
children.

But, now the poorest of the poor is
murdering the unborn in the womb
faster than anyone, especially African
American women, God bless their
souls.
SIRMANS LOG: 19 MAY 2012, 2018
HOURS

A SURE CONSERVATIVE POKER
WINNING HAND IN NOVEMBER 2012
I don't care if my advice is ever taken
seriously; my duty is to keep
pounding out my great wisdom.

Trying to out shout and do attack
damage to a popular liberal is a losing
strategy, mainly because maybe as
much as 95 percent of the American
population is economically ignorant. I
believe less than five percent of
the American people even know or
understand where all government
Income orlglnates from.

Attacking a popular liberal is sort of
like attacking Santa Claus, but, more
and more people are waking up to
Santa Claus spending this nation into
total oblivion. Still, attacking Santa
Claus won't win you a popularly
contest.

My advice is to forget about attacking
someone else and what they have
done or may not do and make sure the
people know what you plan to

do. That is the way Reagan did it. That
is the surest way to defeat a
popular liberal. Otherwise, to keep
attacking and be all over the map no
one will know what to expect from you.

They know at least the sugar daddy
liberals are going to give away the
candy store even if the nation can't
afford it. The only way a conservative
is going to defeat a very popular liberal
in today's climate is to stop all of this
attacking and keep pounding your own
message of lower taxes, more jobs,
and strong national defense and
nothing else.

I'm not running for anything and can't
make anyone take my advice. Polls
and that kind of stuff is a distraction in
itself that the TV pundits and talking
heads gets off on.

The fact is if a conservative just stay
with the said three things and
nothing more until the cows come
home he will win. Otherwise, the poll
distortions and socialist/liberal news
media propaganda attack machine

will make him toast. You see what happened to Dole and McCain, take heed.
SIRMANS LOG: 16 MAY 2012, 2029 HOURS

HOW TO SAVE USA AND GLOBAL ECONOMY:

WILL CIVILIZATION RETURN TO THE STONE AGE?

In life with few exceptions the rule is: "No guts no glory, no risk no gain." There is a simple reason why it is impossible for an economy to work properly when government is too involved. Government acts against the laws of nature, and especially natures' supreme law of "Natural selection."

It's very simple; government stops and prevents the elimination of waste, decay, and inefficiency. You can't have life, growth, or lasting progress being bogged down with waste, decay, and inefficiency. You see, government doesn't adhere to supply and demand;

it operates only on force and power.

Whereas, a free market place economy
with unrestrictive competition
will supply far more than any nation
can use or demand. Believe it or
not, the main reason why is it does
something a pure communist or
socialist system will never do.

Free competition is the stick to get rid
of inefficiency, and allowing an
unlimited individual reward motivates
the most power energy packed force in
our entire human makeup, that energy
force is greed.

People without wisdom and perspective
will never understand this but there is
no other force in our human makeup
with enough motivation to produce
more jobs, food, and everything else
than any one nation can use.

Sure, like electricity greed is very
dangerous, but free competition
bridles it without forceful eliminating or
shutting it down completely like
communism and socialism does. We

use to have this great freedom
in the USA, but with the "New deal"
and our welfare state we are well
on our way to being a communist or
socialist state.

It is simple; there has never been and
never will be a rich and wealthy
country with job for almost everyone
without a lot of greedy rich and
wealthy entrepreneurs to make it
happen. Rich people are not the same
as poor people with money, there is a
world of difference in attitude.

People naturally have different talents
and abilities and should always
have the same opportunity, but to
always receive the same result in life
(reward) is stupid and against the laws
of nature. But, generally that is
what a communist and socialist state
promotes.

That is why government should never
be heavily involved in the
operations of private businesses.
Government is always going to
reward its friend and punish its

perceived enemies. In a democracy
governments job is to collect only
enough taxes to protect the nation
and the upkeep of the infrastructure,
period.

It is not government's duty to be a
social and family provider from cradle
to grave. In my view government as a
social and family provider is like eating
your seed corn or even more horrible
eating your young.

Before the "New deal" government
acting as a nanny state had never
been done on a mass scale in the
history of mankind. It destroys a
nation's culture, nuclear and extended
family system, and any
emergency capacity to barter.

That is a total destruction of the
foundation for human survival;
western
civilization has little left of those 5,000
year pillars of support. When we fall no
one knows where it will end, the Stone
Age is not an impossibility.

Still, with my great wisdom and insight
I'm seen as a nut case, fool, and
a throwback to the eighteenth century
that don't know what the hell I'm
talking about. The only thing I can say
about that is: I pray to God you are
right and I'm wrong. God bless the
USA.
SIRMANS LOG: 15 MAY 2012, 1051
HOURS

JUST LIBERAL PROPAGANDA
BACKGROUND NOISE!
There has never been and never will be
a pure communist or socialist state
that could feed its entire people home
grown without natural resources to
sell. So, to all of these economic
ignorant people that hate capitalism,
rich people, and big business, be
careful of what you wish for because
unless drastic changes are made you
are going to get it.

Unless my deep wisdom advice is
taken which the egg heads will never
do means your wish will be granted
sooner than you think. The reason

is freedom and democracy demands responsibility, accountability, and people with sound judgment, which fewer and fewer has in this great nation today.

Soon when the boom is finally lowered there will only be two choices left, total chaos or total authority, history has shown there will be no compromised middle ground.

Damn, nobody is listening, my God; this dumb idea that one has to refute every single little charge against you in a political race is just plain nonsense. I don't think, in fact I know you can't make hateful negative people like you no matter what you do.

I am a firm believer that if one dwell on doing what he feel is fair and right people of decency and goodwill will accept you for who you are and what you stand for. But, to deny and be overly concerned about every little negative charge by liberals that only want to destroy you is an exercise in futility.

People don't love you because you are
perfect people love you because
you are human caring and decent.
People got eyes, they can see
unfairness from the liberal propaganda
attack machine, and they will
ignore it if the intended victim will
ignore it.

It will be just like water off a ducks
back if one ignores it and keep
pounding low taxes, more jobs, and
strong national defense. Otherwise,
if the intended victim can't ignore it
then the people can't ignore it either
and will detect weakness, which is not
good.

Just make only one statement to any
new charge and get back to pounding
and pounding your message.

Like Nixon said, "The haters can't
destroy you unless you hate them
back, then you destroy yourself." This
lean and mean liberal news
media propaganda attack machine
takes no conservative political

prisoners.

That is just the way it is in this
knockout drag out battle for this
nations
survival as a free nation. This is it
folks, this is for all the marbles, there
will be no tomorrow for individual
freedom in this great nation.

I'm in the fray folks, I don't want to
be, but this is my beloved home the
only home I know. So be it, destiny is
calling on my great wisdom and
perspective.
SIRMANS LOG: 10 MAY 2012, 2359
HOURS

A WELFARE STATE IS LIKE AN
INCESTUOUS RELATIONSHIP!
Economically wise a welfare state may
be compared to an incestuous
relationship. In a normal free market
place economy private enterprise
generate the profit with little to no
government interference.

Through taxing the government takes

off the top only a small cut
needed to protect the nation and
maintain the infrastructure. That way
the economic process and everything
else functions normally.

Nature's supreme law of "Natural
selection" keeps all prices under
control by maintaining a balance
between the merchant and the
consumer. But, in life there is always
going to be people that fall
through the cracks like the poor and
disadvantage.

Throughout history until the "New
deal" came along the nuclear and
extended family system, the church,
and community organizations aided
these people. It was not a perfect
system but it was the best system
known to man for well over six
thousand years.

Just like life itself it had a rebirth and
death cycle known as booms and
busts. Then, here comes liberal do-
gooder geniuses that think they can
take all of the risk out of life. Life can't

exist without risk because there
must be someway to get rid of waste,
decay, and inefficiency. They didn't
realize that nature's supreme law of
"Natural selection" is based on a
survival need for anything to exist over
time.

Now, we as a nation are putting all of
our faith in and depending on one
super sugar daddy provider
government from cradle to grave to
survive. Thereby taking away a
survival need for a system that has
been around well over six thousand
years, how dumb can we get?

More and more there is no survival
need for the once strong nuclear and
extended family, or to have good
morals and values, that is why they
are slowly ceasing out of existence.
There is no wonder why men are
marring men and women are marring
women.

I could go on and on for hours on the
damage the welfare state has
done to our economy, our morals, our

values, and everything else we
use to hold dear. But I will end by
saying: I believe we as a nation are
sc...... ourselves incestuously. Great
solution to the problem is found
throughout my writing and books,
Freddie L. Sirmans, Sr.
SIRMANS LOG: 09 MAY 2012, 1208
HOURS

GOVERNMENT INDIVIDUAL SPENDING
MUST BE KEPT SEPARATE FROM THE
NATION'S ECONOMY IF IT IS TO BE
SAVED.
The reason I pound so hard for
government to separate all of its
individual spending and get the hell
completely out of the nation's free
market place is because that is the
main thing killing our economy.

The stock market and all of that other
stuff is just side issues.
Government involvement is what's
killing the economy that is why I
stress so hard that government must
start using tokens or script when
aiding the poor and disadvantage on

an individual basis.

That will prevent government spending
from contaminating the national
economy. Sure, we must not let people
freeze and starve but the only way
government can aid the poor and
disadvantage without destroying
the free market place economy is by
operating its own commissaries,
housing, and clinics system with the
use of tokens or script to keep that
spending separate.

The destructive system we are using
now takes tax money from one
group of Americans, and then in
competition against we the tax payers
gives that money to another less
producing group which results in
higher and higher prices and taxes on
everyone.

That is why tokens or script must be
used for all government spending
that is done on an individual basis, that
would keep merchants from raising
prices higher and higher on everyone,
which is the reason for the consumer

inflation we have today.

The main way this contamination
occurs is when government gives out
masses amounts of money on an
individual basis. That infusion of mass
amount of unearned (government
spending is unearned spending)
money allows merchant to raising
prices higher and higher against
ourselves we the tax payers.

The government subsides price raising
on everyone by giving out masses
amount of money and food stamps to
the poor and
disadvantage on an individual basis,
there is not enough rich and others
to support too high prices.

Without that government subsidy to
the poor and disadvantage, basic
food and medical prices could never go
higher than the poor could
afford.

So, instead of subsiding higher prices
on everyone in helping the poor, the
poor and disadvantage can still be

helped without the government
driving up prices, if only government
would use tokens or script in its
own government operated support
systems.

Making the government use tokens of
script for all individual government
spending would stop this nonsense, as
you see, economic ignorance is staring
us in the face.

So, in closing this chapter, I repeat, for
this nation and our economy to
survive all government spending done
on an individual basis tokens or script
must be used, period. God! I ask in
you name, save our great nation.
SIRMANS LOG: 08 MAY 2012, 0958
HOURS

CAUTION! CONSERVATIVES THINK
BEFORE YOU LEAP!
Warning! Stop! Don't! For now don't
cut or reduce spending or anything
else. It will only reduce the size of the
pie and make everything worse
and maybe even instantly wreck the

economy.

A smaller pie means fewer jobs and everything else, and it may even double the dole population and push the debt from 16 trillion to 32 trillion. Government spending ain't the problem it is how it is doing the spending.

It shouldn't but if government is going to do social and provider spending anyway it should be done by providing government commissaries, government housing, and government clinic with the use of tokens or script.

Government get the hell out of private enterprise and let private enterprise and the free market place sink or swim on its own, this is an order. To kick start and get this whole process rolling right now eliminate the minimum wage.

The welfare state era is over. Government in the role of social and family provider has out lived its time. Profit from American businesses

is the only thing that supports our
government either from directly
taxing business or indirectly from the
wages paid to business employees and
their property.

Let's describe business profit as your
seed corn. When government is small
and taking care of only national
defense and infrastructure like parks,
roads, and bridges it only needs to
take a small amount of business seed
corn profit. That way the business will
have plenty left to raise and grow
another bumper crop.

But, when government takes on a
social and family provider role it
rapidly grows government demanding
it take bigger and bigger chunks
of businesses seed corn profit. The
bigger chunk government takes the
less seed corn the business will have to
grow another crop.

Our government welfare state as social
and family provider now has
grown so large there is not enough
business seed corn profit available

for the welfare state to take to survive
without killing off American
business. That is what this liberal
created social and family provider
government has brought this great
nation too.

There is no foreign invader, we are
now face to face with the enemy,
and it is economic ignorance. We are
now at economic death door, we
no longer have a choice, we either
separate all government spending
from our free enterprise economic
system or the economy will definitely
collapse and freedom in this nation will
be lost forever.

This can be done by the government
not giving anyone money unless
they work for the government, also no
food stamps. Of course the
government must help people and not
let people freeze or starve.

But, government must do that by
operating government run
commissaries, housing, and clinics with
the use of tokens or script, but there

must be a separation, otherwise it will
be impossible for our less than free
market place economy to survive.

Also, we must as a nation eliminates
the minimum wage, that way the
people can save themselves. A half a
loaf is better than nothing because
all of the supposedly safety nets won't
have the funds to save anyone.
It coming folks, this government is
broke and the sooner that sinks in
the better.

Right now to the masses of
government dependents that kind of
talk about economic failure is just
pesky noise. Lord save this great
nation. Folks, I know my drum beat to
eliminate the minimum wage don't
seem to make sense, but I have the
wisdom and perspective to know it is
the only way out.

A minimum wage is a forced
manipulation of the free market which
means we don't have a free market
place economy. If we did we wouldn't
be in the sad shape we are in. Without

a forced minimum wage the whole economy would be in balance.

With no minimum wage labor and cost would balance each other allowing the very poor to afford and pay their own food and medical bills, which now is impossible. The minimum wage ain't free, people don't realize it but it just forces a business to charge more for everything you buy.

Sure, in moderation a higher wage is not a bad thing, but when has a government handout ever stopped with moderation. Besides, it is done by force and that is totally against the rules of a free market place economy.
SIRMANS LOG: 7 MAY 2012, 1527 HOURS

CURRENT EVENT INJECTION: 3 MAY 2012, 2333
HOURS
Whoa! Maybe I'm crazy and it's just me! Or maybe I'm just missing something here! Or maybe it's just a

liberal thing! When did we as a
nation become proud to air our dirty
linen in public! Sure, sometimes
you gotta do what you gotta do, but,
who says you have to publically
wallow in it? What happened, it has
always been the American way to
use a big stick and walk silently.
CURRENT EVENT INJECTION END:
SIRMANS LOG: 3 MAY 2012, 2345
HOURS

UPDATED: 2 MAY 2012, 1827 HOURS
THE MIGHTY LIBERAL PROPAGANDA
ATTACK
MACHINE IN ACTION IS AN AWESOME
POWER!
The big horse race coming up in
November in my view will determine
the survival of western civilization. To
take the golden crown for the
conservatives it is going to take a no
holds barred knock down drag out
political battle like no one has ever
seen in this country.

Get the women, children, and old folks
off the streets, which, I'm sure,

disqualifies me and my views up front.
Standing between whoever
takes the crown is a dug in hardcore
battle harden predominate liberal
news media that sees self-sufficiency
and old fashion traditional family
values as the enemy.

The all powerful liberal news media has
brain washed ninety five
percent of the American people to
some degree to believe the welfare
state will always be around to take
care of everybody instead of every
man feeling responsible for his own
survival.

The might of the liberal propaganda
machine aimed at any conservative
is an awesome sight of raw power.
When it hits a conservative even
some hardcore conservatives may ease
up and not speak as freely their
true convictions, let alone pretenders
who may end up trying to out liberal a
liberal.

No matter how many so called power
brokers bet on the horse they think

can take the crown it ain't gonna happen unless that horse hold to conservative values. The biggest weakness of the all powerful liberal news media propaganda attack machine is their conviction that they are right and that most Americans agree with them.

They are dead wrong on that, as a rule whatever the liberal news media believes the American people believe just the opposite. But, people are human and when they are bombarded and pounded over and over with the same liberal propaganda it has an effect. And it will carry the day, especially it you don't have a genuine conservative with the guts to push back tit for tat.

With the liberal attack machine constant on guard ready to pounce, the smartest thing any conservative can do is select only about three things to dwell on and nothing more.

Sure, it will get boring and people will

be saying I know that and I am
tired of hearing that and they may
tune out but they won't forget the
three things you stand for, otherwise
being all over the map the liberal
propaganda attack machine will make
sure no one knows what the hell
you stand for.

Grab a sound bite for lower taxes,
better job opportunities, and keeping
a strong national defense. Just like a
pit bull bite down on those three
things and never ease up come hell or
high waters.

If a conservative keep it simple and
refuse to get dispersed all over the
map he will take the crown. But, if he
starts watching all of the polls
and listening to all of the liberal
defeatist propaganda he may start
thinking and acting like a loser, which
can then become a reality.

I've seen in action the awesome power
of the liberal propaganda attack
machine in taking out Dole and then
McCain, and believe me the stage is

set for a repeat. Even now no one can really tell you what either of those candidates truly stood for, pro or con, simply because they were all over the map.

The only way to get through this mine field is to keep it simple, bore the hell out of the people with not more than three proven conservative winners. Like the old football technique, "Three and a half yards and a cloud of dust," everybody in the stands knew what you were going to do but the opposition couldn't stop you.

The same applies here, Pound and pound sound bites on low taxes, more jobs, and strong nation defense and nothing else until the cows come home. Otherwise, the liberal propaganda attack machine will disperse your message and label you to their liking and smash you like a bug.

It is a mine game; too, the attack machine armed with polls, the special interest, and others will be hollering

and whooping it up to pry you loose
from those three proven winners.

Like any winning coach will tell you,
you can never guarantee you will win,
the most you can do in any game is be
in a position to win, then the odds are
in your favor because on a given day
luck is as much a part of the game as
anything else.

And For-God-Sake forget about details,
all that does is give the liberal
propaganda attack machine fodder and
ammo for propaganda to confirm the
cold heartless uncaring label they are
trying to make stick.

Just layout the three things you are
going to do and keep pounding
them until the cows come home. How
you are going to do this and how
are you going to do that will only be
taken out of context and distorted
to drown out your real massages.

Forget about reasoning, you can't
reason with liberals, they don't care
about logic and reason; their only care

is to win in anyway and at any
cost. A genuine responsible person
would self-sacrifice and put country
above all personal interest, but with
the shape this country is in all the
blame can't be placed just on liberals.

In fact ninety five percent of the
general population in the country is
still asleep with unshakable faith in
uncle sugar and has no idea of the
dire shape this country is in, our
freedom and way of life is at deaths
door and less then five percent of the
population even realize it. Lord,
have mercy on our souls.

Sure, the Madison Avenue boys and
girls along with the party pollster's
and experts will be totally against what
I am saying, but, I stand by my
analysis.

Trying to out shout and stay one upper
on a liberal tends not to work because
subconsciously people know that
generally liberals lack a very deep
sense of responsibility. And they tend
not to hold liberals to as high a

standard as a conservative.

The independents will never desert one that will stick only to low taxes, more jobs, and strong national defense if they know he is sincere. But, to be lured off into chasing after women issues, gay issues, who killed who, and every other Tom, Dick, and Harry liberal outcry imaginable is just what the liberal attack machine wants.

The sensible thing to do with a new outcry is make only one policy statement, and stand by it by telling the distractors my first statement stands. Then get back to pounding and pounding low taxes, more jobs, and a strong national defense. Otherwise, the liberal propaganda attack machine will keep you away from your bread and butter message forever

Whoa here! I hear more liberal claptrap, this anti wealth mentality that
is in the liberal mind is just that, because it just doesn't pan out in

practice. There is something in the makeup of the human psyche that attracts people to bigger than life stuff.

For some unknown reason pomp, ceremony, extravaganza, and all of that kind of crazy nonessential stuff have an attraction and pulling effect on people. I really don't know why, but I suspect that it has something to do with the allure of power. There is just something that attracts people to that kind of stuff.

Look at all of the worshiping of movie stars and big time sport figures. Evangelism is big business in this country today with mega-churches, but one of the lessons learned by the early evangelist was how to build a big following.

They learned that one could be the best preacher with the best message and that alone may get you some followers, but it took more to build a Hugh following. And one effective way was to be seen as bigger than life with pomp, expensive flashy cars, fine pews, fine churches & furniture, and fine flashy clothes.

I think most seniors have heard of Daddy Grace and other early evangelist. So, all I'm saying is living high on the hog doesn't necessarily turn most people off. Who it actually turns off is those with a something for nothing socialist mentality.

The reason I wrote this article is because the socialist/liberal news media propaganda attack machine was trying to stir up resentment among the people, because someone with their own hard earned money was proud of the cars they could afford.

Poor hard working Americans has never resented rich people enjoying the good life. In fact they want that, too. In America anything is still possible, that is if we can keep these socialist from taking over.

Just remember the story about the Woodchopper; he was trying to split an extra tough might oak block. He hit

the blade of his big axe time and
time again on this particular block.
After a while he felt there was no
use and decided to give up.

But, at the last minute before walking
away he decided to kneel down
and take a closer look. And to his
surprise he could see a small split.
The moral of the story is: Positive
human effort is never wasted. Many
times we may feel it doesn't really
matter and we are just wasting our
time on something.

So many times over the years with my
writing I have felt it is a curse, I
haven't made any money at it, and felt
nobody really cares and it all a
waste of time. But, the thing with me
is I don't know how to be a quitter
and I'm still at it.

All of my life I have been written off
dismissed and seen as someone
destiny to be a failure in life, but, by
the grace of God here I am still
standing at age seventy, three days
before this Christmas 2012.

As you can see, I am in favor of
restoring old fashion values to this
nation, I may not be right, but this is
my analysis on what it will take to
grab the golden crown and save
western civilization.
SIRMANS LOG: 21 APRIL 2012, 1806
HOURS

READ MY SHORT RAW NO CHASER
LECTURE ON SIRMANS ECONOMICS!
It never ceases to amaze me on just
how economically ignorant most
people are. This whole modern
generation is looking to big
government
to always be there to take care of
them. But, the true fact is the
government is only a necessary
parasite that every organized society
must have to defend and protect its
citizens.

An Economy consists of only to parties,
a seller and a buyer or a merchant and
a consumer. Nature's supreme law of
"Natural selection" balances these two

forces against each other where prices
can never get out of hand.

If government just take a small
amount off the top a balance can still
be
maintained, but, when government
takes too much of the cream of
profit the incentive to produce heads
downward. The government
doesn't generate any profit and every
penny it takes in taxes to survive
originates from some form of private
business transaction.

It is either directly or indirectly. Non
business people that pay taxes to
the government all receive their pay
from some form of private
business transaction profit. So, what
have we now, a general public
that see government as some kind of
imaginary omnipotent sow with
countless tits that we can suck on
forever.

Besides, a business doesn't pay taxes
anyway; a business is just a medium
of exchange and nothing else. It is a

medium of exchange between a buyer
and a seller with the seller being the
owner of the product or service. The
exchange between the seller (owner)
and the buyer must produce a profit
for the owner otherwise all of the
owner's
labor would be for nothing.

So, when the government comes in
and taxes the owner's profit that tax
must be passed on to the buyer
(customer) in the form of higher
prices.
You see, when the government taxes a
business it is simply indirectly
taxing the public or a part of it in the
form of higher prices, that is what
is called consumer inflation.

When the tax is small there is not
much of a problem, but when the bite
becomes too great especially along
with mountains of government red
tape, unemployment and mass
business failure is the result.

That is sheer madness and to top that
we have this liberal anti-business

climate that bites the hand that feeds it. My God! It is a case of the parasite attacking the host that keeps it alive, how dumb and stupid can it get? This is what the shallow minded liberals and their welfare state has done to this great predominate Christian nation.

There has never been a mass social and family provider government in the history of mankind before the "New deal" came along. The profits from private enterprise are what supports government and can keep government supplied as long as government limits its spending to national defense and the infrastructure.

But, the profit from private business can never be enough to support a social and provider government very long. The welfare state days are over, it is no mystery to me, there is simply not enough business profit to pay the cost, and you can't get blood out of a turnip, period. And anybody that think that we as a nation can continue with our welfare state is living in fantasy land, period.

It is simply impossible to pay the cost,
we are broke people, and still we
have politicians in washing acting like
we are a rich nation. We are over
16 trillion in debt and still trying to
spend like drunken sailors.

The egg heads with their scrambled
brains and the elite will never
change course they are in a state of
denial and will go down with the
ship first. Why they call them
eggheads in the first place is because
their brains are scrambled, with
common sense nowhere to be found.
And I'm supposed to be the fool and
nut case and maybe I am, but at least
I have enough common sense to know
we are headed toward total
doom.

I write what I think and believe, so I
hope my short lecture will enlighten at
least one soul somewhere out there
and everyone won't think I am totally
insane.

When I talk about economics I'm talking about a free market place. There has never been a communist or socialist form of government that could feed all of it people. In those types of governments the top leadership lives high on the hog while the general population barley keeps from starving.
SIRMANS LOG: 30 MARCH 2012, 0017 HOURS

QUICK WORD OF KNOWLEDGE INJECTION:
Economically speaking caring for the poor or anybody must be kept separated for a free market place to work, that is the problem now, you can't have unlimited individual government spending standing between the merchants and the consumers and expect a healthy sound free
market place economy. What you will have is uncontrolled consumer inflation like what is taking place now, that and the "Minimum wage" is the fuel that is spinning consumer

inflation out of control.

There is no way in the hell to stop this economy from expanding beyond control and collapse from it own weight with the course it is on. You don't have to take my advice; the wait won't be very much longer. Government must sell off damn near everything and give up its social and family provider role, period. Will it happen, no?

If the USA government doesn't eliminate the "Minimum wage and give up its social and family provider role will the USA economy survive, no. So, what is going to happen to this great land of the free and home of the brave, you really don't want to know the answer to that as I see it.

Well, if you insist and won't take no for an answer I guess I have no choice but to tell you what I think is going to happen. I believe to buy time and avoid biting the dust our Welfare State and the Federal Reserve as co-conspirators will finish selling off what is left of our

freedom and sovereignty to some
foreign highest bidder like a cheap
street walker. And we will end up as
debt slaves.

So, how you like me now?
SIRMANS LOG: Last update 27 MARCH
2012, 1613 HOURS

THE END

BY FREDDIE L. SIRMANS, SR.
WEBSITE: www.FLSirmans.com